Grannies, Inc.
Guide to Knitting

Grannies, Inc. Guide to Knitting

LEARN TIPS & TECHNIQUES FROM THE BEST

KATIE MOWAT

EBURY
PRESS

10 9 8 7 6 5 4 3 2 1

Published in 2012 by Ebury Press, an imprint of Ebury Publishing

A Random House Group Company

Text © Katie Mowat 2012
Photography © Ebury Press 2012

Katie Mowat has asserted her right to be identified as the author of this
Work in accordance with the Copyright, Designs and Patents Act 1988

The Random House Group Limited Reg. No. 954009

Addresses for companies within the Random House Group can be found at
www.randomhouse.co.uk

A CIP catalogue record for this book is available from the British Library

The Random House Group Limited supports The Forest Stewardship
Council® (FSC®), the leading international forest certification organisation.
Our books carrying the FSC label are printed on FSC® certified paper. FSC is
the only forest certification scheme endorsed by the leading environmental
organisations, including Greenpeace. Our paper procurement policy can be
found at www.randomhouse.co.uk/environment

To buy books by your favourite authors and register for offers visit
www.randomhouse.co.uk

Design by Pettibone Design
Photography by Brent Darby
Illustrations by Kate Simunek

Printed and bound in China by Toppan Leefung

ISBN 9780091943615

I would like to dedicate this book to all the knitting grannies out there, without whom I would never have had the inspiration for Grannies, Inc. and this book. It is your talent and intrinsic knowledge of knitting that fuels my determination to keep this outlet for creativity, individualism and craft alive in my generation and many more to come.

Contents

If I'm Sittin' I'm Knittin'

20 Patterns to Keep Your Fingers Busy **112**

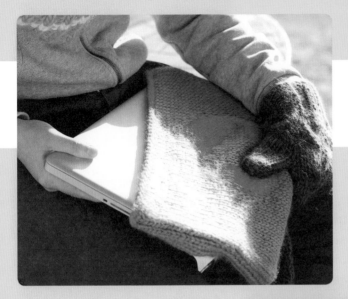

Needles Down, Feet Up

Stuff that wasn't Around in
Our Day **180**

Introduction:
There's Wisdom in the Wool

I picked up knitting while studying at the University of California, Santa Cruz, where the craft had become something of a craze – most likely due to the number of celebrities reported to be doing it (Julia Roberts, Madonna and even Russell Crowe).

I was fascinated by the ability to design my own woolly accessories and felt somewhat privileged that I could also knit them into reality. With an emerging market for bespoke fashion and even more demand for ethical fashion, the idea for my design-your-own fashion label was born.

After recruiting the first knitters by putting a small ad on a knitting website, I soon realised that the responses I got back were mainly from ladies of the older generation who had been knitting for decades and had literally run out of people to knit for. The idea was complete. I was going to offer the nation the unique chance of designing their own beanie and have it knitted, especially for them, by an eagerly awaiting granny. From the initial beanie design we rapidly expanded to a whole range of accessories. The 15 core grannies who work for Grannies, Inc. are all overflowing with ideas and have a deep, unrivalled knowledge of knitting.

In the *Grannies, Inc. Guide to Knitting*, the grannies and I will dispense plenty of advice on the art of hand knitting and share with you some techniques you'll need to customise our patterns, aimed at inspiring all levels of knitter. We'll talk you through every step of creating your one-off pieces, from choosing the type of wool to different stitch options to edging and finishing techniques. All along the way our grannies will be there to pass on their expert knowledge founded on 50+ years of experience through purls of wisdom, so be sure to look out for these.

So what are you waiting for? Pick up those needles and get ready to flex those creative muscles...

Katie Mowat
Founder of Grannies, Inc.

How to Get Started
LET THE STASHING BEGIN

Yarn

The variety of yarns available to the hand knitter never fails to astound us. Every time we visit our local yarn shops they have a new array of wonderful samples to show us. If you took a peek in any seasoned knitter's yarn stash you'd most probably find a huge variety of yarns of differing fibres and weights, colours and textures. Yarn can get quite addictive, so we warn you now that once you start, you'll forever be adding to your stash and before you know it you'll have yarn coming out of your ears!

It's nothing to be afraid of though – there is no better feeling than making something out of the scraps of unused yarn you bought 40 years ago. And it also gives you the chance to try out oodles of ideas as your knitting expertise grows. Here at Grannies, Inc. we try out patterns in a multitude of yarns to see what kind of results we get – and we urge you to do the same. The patterns in this book are designed to be flexible, so make them your own by mixing up the type of yarns you use for them. This section is intended to familiarise you with the types of yarn available and to guide you in how to adapt patterns to your yarn choices.

Good Yarn Comes in Many Packages

One of the first things you have to get your head around is the number of different packages in which yarn comes. There are generally three different ways in which manufacturers present their yarns and these are by balling, skeining or hanking.

Back in the day, all yarn was provided in hanks and it was the job of husbands and children to hold out the hanks, stretched between their two hands while the ladies balled the yarn by hand, ready to knit with. It's the classic picture.

To make a hank the yarn is wound into a large ring shape (in the olden days this was done using a funny contraption called a 'niddy noddy') and then twisted until it is folded back on itself. Hanks are becoming more and more popular by way of yarn packaging, so get ready to start balling!

A skein of yarn is probably what you think of when you picture yarn in your head. Yarn is wound into an oblong shape in a way that some clever person came up with to allow the end of it to be pulled from either the inside of the ball or the outside. (Pulling yarn from the inside of the ball will stop it jumping up and down and rolling around at your feel as you're knitting.)

A ball of yarn is a just as you would imagine – a-ball-of-yarn. The yarn is wound into a ball and the knitter pulls the yarn from outside to knit with it (or sometimes from the inside, if you're lucky).

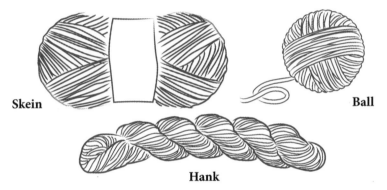

Skein

Ball

Hank

Natural Fibres – Soft, Soft, Soft!

Grannies, Inc. would always recommend using higher-quality natural fibres for accessory patterns in order to produce soft, luxurious results. If you're going to put the time and love into hand knitting an item, you might as well use the best-quality yarn, no?

Natural yarns are made from either animal or vegetable fibres and in themselves differ greatly. You'll be able get a good feel for the softness and texture of different types of yarn just by touch, but your choice of yarn will also affect the elasticity of your finished item, the way it falls and how easy it will be care for, so it's good to bear these qualities in mind when deciding on which to buy.

Natural Fibres

Fibre	Source	Characteristics
Alpaca	Coat of the alpaca, close relation to the llama	Very soft and lustrous, similar to cashmere but generally cheaper. Hardwearing and keeps its shape well.
Angora	Hair of the Angora rabbit	Very furry and likely to shed. Light and delicate, making it hard to care for. Drapes well but has little elasticity.
Bamboo	Fibres of the bamboo plant	Eco-fibre with natural anti-allergic, anti-bacterial and temperature-balancing properties. Has a natural sheen like silk and is as soft and comfortable as cashmere.
Cashmere	Underhair of the Kashmir goat	Very expensive but really soft and luxurious. Lightweight and keeps its shape well.
Cotton	Ball of the cotton plant	Heavy, but often blended with other fibres to lighten it, which makes it perfect for summer garments. Doesn't keep its shape well.
Linen	Stem of the flax plant	Rougher than other fibres and often blended with cotton to soften. Drapes well and works well for lightweight garments.
Mohair	Coat of the Angora goat	Light and highly textured with a tendency to shed. Very soft and resilient.
Silk	Fibres of the silkworm larvae cocoon	Highly lustrous, soft and light. Low elasticity and tends to pill.
Wool	Fleece of a sheep	Varies greatly depending on which sheep it comes from, with Merino being amongst the finest and softest. Warm and breathable with excellent insulating properties.

Synthetic Fibres

Most often made from acrylic, polyester, nylon and viscose, synthetic yarns are cheaper than natural ones but are of a lesser quality. They are available in a wide range of colours and textures and are generally easier to care for than natural fibres. As well as lacking in elasticity, they are usually pretty bad at retaining heat; so for winter accessories, don't even think about it!

Weight and Plies

So, you remember that yarn stash we told you about earlier? Well, you can be sure that not only will a knitter's stash be full of different yarn fibres, but it is also sure to be oozing with different weights of yarn, with different plies. You see, yarn is either made up of a single strand of fibre (called a ply) or a number of strands twisted together, and the thickness of the yarn is dependent on how tightly the individual strands are spun, rather than the number of plies.

It is very important to understand yarn weights, as they are the basis on which all patterns are created; if you want to be adventurous and try out different yarns, it essential that you know how to choose substitutes that will work in the pattern.

> **GRANNY'S PURL OF WISDOM**
>
> So you don't punish your purse, or choose a difficult material to care for, you can use a blended yarn. There are endless blends of both natural and synthetic fibres available, all of which retain the features of the higher-quality fibres while adding more practical properties, such as being machine washable.

Most yarns can be categorised into six common weights, all of which are explained overleaf. Once you have learned these you're bound to start spotting them everywhere in your everyday life and begin identifying them to yourself with inner pride. I've also included the usual tension and recommended needle size for each weight (which should make sense once you've read the next section: 'All the Gear and

No Idea', page 30) so that you're not having to flick all around the place when you need to reference these in the future.

2PLY

TENSION: 27-32sts • NEEDLE SIZE: 2¼-3¼mm

See how that ply knowledge is already coming into use? 2ply weight yarn is simply two strands (plies) of yarn twisted together. Easy. It's great for garments that need very accurate fitting, such as gloves and socks.

4PLY

TENSION: 23-26sts • NEEDLE SIZE: 3¼-3¾mm

Again, a wonderfully simple name so you really know where you stand. Go on, have a guess as to how many plies are involved in this one then? It is thicker than the 2ply, although our earlier lesson in plies has taught us that the higher the number of plies does not necessarily mean a thicker yarn. This one is a favourite for baby clothes and lacy garments.

DOUBLE KNITTING (DK)

TENSION: 21-24sts • NEEDLE SIZE: 3¾-4½mm

Now this one takes a little bit of thinking, but not much. Double Knitting is most commonly referred to by its abbreviation – 'DK' – and is named as such because it is double the weight of 4ply. DK is used all over the place and is arguably the most widely used yarn. Its versatility means that it is great for all kinds of garments, so we think it would be unfair to suggest what it is best for because it could handle just about anything!

ARAN

TENSION: 16-20sts • NEEDLE SIZE: 4½-5½mm

Oh, we could go on and on about the history of the Aran-weight yarn – it's fascinating! It was named after a style of knitting that originated in the Aran Isles, six miles off the west coast of Ireland. Tradition has it that the original jumpers knitted using this weight of yarn incorporated stitch patterns that could identify a drowned fisherman if lost at sea.

That said, nowadays it's best used for jumpers and other garments that require a thicker alternative to DK.

CHUNKY

TENSION: 12-15sts • NEEDLE SIZE: 5½-8mm

Does what it says on the tin, this one. Chunky yarn produces chunky knits that are perfect for winter outdoor wear, such as oversized cardies, scarves and beanies. We have to admit that this weight is our favourite at the moment, as it's produced such warm and comforting garments. This is also one we'd recommend to newbies, because you'll see results much quicker than with the finer yarns, which will really pay off after all your hard grind!

SUPER CHUNKY

TENSION: 16-11sts • NEEDLE SIZE: 8mm+

We love the name of this weight – doesn't it just make you want to jump into a pile of it? Super chunky is getting rather popular these days and it's understandable why. It's the ultimate quick-knit and is great for beginners as it's possible to get a whole scarf knit in a single day. Try scarves, snoods and home textiles such as cushion covers – the texture will be unbelievable.

Just to add a little complexity to these yarn weights, you should probably know about some alternative names for them, as different countries and different designers have their own quirky way of describing yarn weights that can often confuse the learner knitter:

Yarn Weights

UK Name	Alternative Names
4ply	Sport, Baby
DK	Light Worsted
Aran	Worsted, Fisherman
Chunky	Bulky
Super Chunky	Super Bulky

Texture

Just to add a few more options to your already vast choice of yarns, textured yarns are definitely worth a mention. There are so many different textured yarns out there and the trend seems to be changing all the time – we can hardly keep up! We advise you to have your finger on the pulse to keep up with the novelty yarn 'du jour', but the following few have been firmly on the scene for a while now, so I'd be happy to tell you about them without sounding dated.

Mohair/Angora Both mohair and Angora fibres make highly textured yarns that consist of a fine core strand with fluffy strands coming off it (caused by brushing). These are best knit on larger needles than their weight and metreage would imply as the fluffy strands fill the loose stitches, creating a very light piece of fabric. Because of their fluffy nature these yarns can be itchy when worn very close to the skin, so it is best that you knit them in patterns designed for looser garments.

Chenille A seriously velvety, short-pile yarn. Since learning that 'chenille' is the French word for caterpillar, whenever we knit with it we imagine passing one long fuzzy caterpillar through our fingers with its short hairs tickling our palms as we go. Have a go yourself, it's strangely enjoyable!

Slub Well, what a name. We just love it! It sounds so onomatopoeic, but unfortunately not. Slub is a yarn spun unevenly so that it forms lumps (aptly called 'slubs'). We're thinking that originally it was just a way for spinners to sell their 'mistakenly' uneven yarns, which the arty knitter then adopted as a yarn in its own right. Very savvy business folk those spinners.

Tape/Ribbon As expected, these yarns are flat like a piece of tape or ribbon, of course! With extra care they can be knitted without any

twists, but if you can't be bothered just go with it and let the yarn fold and twist as you knit (we actually prefer the resulting fabric with these 'imperfections').

Tweed Oh, this does remind us of our school days and those lovely green tweed blazers! Tweed is a mottled yarn with one dominant colour flecked with other colours to give it an uneven texture. It looks strong and warm when knitted into a garment, like it can take on any weather conditions thrown at it!

Colour

And you thought your choice ended at texture, didn't you? Nope. One last little bit you need to think about when it comes to choosing yarn is colour – and personally it's our favourite bit (but we promise not to waffle on and bore you).

As Joseph and his multi-coloured wonder-coat would probably agree, colour is king. Everyone's a little happier with colour in their life and wardrobe, so think carefully when selecting yarn for a project. Everybody has different opinions about which colours they like and whether they believe colour clashing is 'in vogue' or 'so 2000 and late' (to coin a phrase from The Black Eyed Peas). Some people like to colour it up to the max, as if they'd just walked straight out of a rainbow, and others like to goth it down, totally covering themselves in black. Well, that's up to you, I'm a big advocate of individualism, but let me just give you a couple of things to think about when choosing yarn...

You can buy yarn either dyed or undyed. Undyed yarn takes on the colour of the animal's fibre in its natural state and can vary greatly depending on the animal and breed.

> **GRANNY'S PURL OF WISDOM**
>
> Don't bother trying to knit an intricate stitch pattern with highly textured yarn – it just won't work! The pattern will get lost in the yarn and you'll not be able to see all of that lovely detail you worked so hard to produce. Best to stick to smoother yarns for complex patterns.

We think it is safe to say, though, that most yarns on the market are dyed (using natural or artificial dyes) to give them a single, uniform colour. The range of colours is unending, so if you're looking for a specific hue you're bound to find it somewhere.

You can use more than one colour in a garment by joining in new colours part-way through and weaving in the ends (see 'How to Knit' on page 72), however there is another way to add multiple colours, and that is by using a variegated yarn:

- **Heathers or tweed** Yarn with flecks of a different-coloured fibre.
- **Ombre** Yarn with lighter and darker shades of a single hue.
- **Multi-coloured** Yarn with more than one distinct hue (a 'parrot colourway' might have green, yellow and red).

- **Self-striping** Yarn dyed with lengths of colour that blend into each other and will repeatedly create stripes in a knitted fabric.
- **Marled** Yarn made from twisting a number of different-coloured plies together.

Where to buy the bloomin' stuff

In this busy day and age it's a wonder anyone ever manages to get to their local yarn shop, but if you can, we recommend you do. You'll be inspired. As a newbie it's important to feel the yarn and get to know the different textures and qualities available, and your yarn shop should encourage this. We might be biased, but knitters are lovely people and those who run yarn shops are extra special. Don't be afraid: ask them questions, ask their advice, ask for a discount (!) – they'll be keen as a bean to help you out and might even take the time to sit down and help you conquer that damned stitch you've been pondering over for weeks.

Your next best bet for buying yarn is on the internet. There are obvious advantages of doing this over visiting your local shop in terms of variety and (generally) price, but beware that it is very difficult to represent correct colours on a computer screen so you'll have to be a little flexible when it comes to that. There is also no substitute for actually touching the yarn with your fingertips to know it's the one for you. It's worth noting, though, that in the UK it is your legal right, according to Distance Selling Regulations, to send your yarn back within a week of it being delivered for a full refund (including outward delivery charges), even if there's no fault. You will most probably have to pay for the return postage, though, so do weigh up all these factors before purchasing yarn online.

Lastly, if you haven't done so already, we would recommend you visit a yarn fair or exhibition, which are held fairly regularly throughout the year in many different countries. It is such a luxury for us to visit a fair every now and again, where we always find the most beautiful, 'under-the-radar' yarns and very often get to meet the spinners and dyers ourselves. It's a real treat – give it a go. Our favourite UK fairs are listed on page 168, however with the increase in popularity that the craft of hand knitting has seen over the past decade, there are bound to be additions to this list every year. A simple internet search should reveal an up-to-date list for any part of the world.

Reading a Yarn Label

Yarn labels, or ball bands, have loads of helpful information that knitters can use to make decisions on what to buy for their projects. Some can be more informative than others, but in general the following details should always be conveyed somewhere on the label.

Fibre content Remember all those different types of fibre used to make yarn that we mentioned earlier? Well, bring that information to the front of your mind when reading yarn labels, because picking the right fibre will most probably be one of the first decisions you'll need to make when choosing a yarn.

Weight Most patterns should indicate an approximate weight of yarn that you need to complete a project, so make sure you buy enough at the start. Note that different fibres have different weights, so if you're substituting a yarn in place of the one mentioned in the pattern, it's best to check the metreage rather than buy the same weight as yarn that the pattern recommends.

Metreage or yardage If you're being adventurous and opting for a yarn other than the one used in the pattern you'll need to know the metreage of it so you can work out how much yarn you need to buy. If the metreage is the same (or very similar) to the one in the pattern, you're safe to buy as much as the pattern suggests. If it is different, divide the total metreage required in the pattern by the metreage of the substitute yarn ball to determine how much to buy (always round up). That'll save you another trip to the shops or online delivery charge.

Recommended needle size and tension Most yarn manufacturers will recommend a knitting needle size for making a solid fabric using their yarn. This is only a recommendation, though, so don't be afraid to ignore it when you're feeling experimental. The tension is what is most important for your project. You must adjust your tension to match the pattern you are using to ensure sizing is correct, but don't worry about this for now, we'll teach you how to do that later on. The only thing you need to know at this point is that the funny grid symbol on the label signifies the tension of an average knitter using the recommended needle size.

Dye lot and colour Generally yarn is dyed after it is spun, in batches called 'dye lots'. If yarn is dyed in this way its label should provide you with a dye lot number so that when buying multiple balls for a project you can make sure they all come from the same dye lot and thereby avoid slight variations in colour. (This is also why it is best to be generous with the amount of yarn you buy for a project as you can't guarantee you'll be able to find the same dye lot a month later when you've run out.) The yarn label should also have a colour name or number, which is helpful if you need to buy more yarn or just like it so much that you want to use it for another project.

Care advice Just as clothing bears care symbols to make sure you don't ruin it in the wash, so too does yarn. Which is obvious when you think about it. Each of us can recall the feeling of our heart breaking after pulling a garment out of the washing machine we had spent months making, only to discover it had shrunk to a doll's size. We beg you all to take these care instructions very seriously when it comes to hand knitting and never double-think the manufacturer – they know best!

If you are knitting for someone else it is a good idea to keep the ball band and give it to them with the finished piece for them to refer to when cleaning the garment. If in doubt, always hand wash knitted items in cold water and lie them flat to dry – that's our motto!

Care Instructions

Wash by hand.		A single bar beneath the wash tub indicates medium washing conditions at the stated temperature. Designed specifically for machine-washable synthetic products.	
A wash tub without a bar indicates maximum washing conditions may be used at the temperature stated. Designed specifically for machine-washable cotton products.		A double underline beneath the wash tub indicates minimum washing conditions at the stated temperature. Designed specifically for machine-wash able wool products.	

May be tumble dried:		…at a low heat setting.	
…at a high heat setting		Do not tumble dry.	

Any bleach allowed.	Only oxygen bleach/ non-chlorine bleach allowed.	No bleach allowed.	

Hot iron.	Warm iron.	Cool iron.	

Must be professionally dry cleaned. The letters contained within the circle and/or a bar beneath the circle will indicate the solvent and the process to be used by the dry cleaner.	Must be professionally dry cleaned. The letters contained within the circle and/or a bar beneath the circle will indicate the solvent and the process to be used by the dry cleaner.	
Professional wet clean only.	Do not dry clean.	

A cross through any symbol means 'DO NOT'	

Adapting Patterns to Different Yarns

One of the biggest attractions to knitting for us is the ability to create individual pieces and customise patterns to exactly our own tastes. One of the easiest ways to do this is to experiment with yarn. Many knitters are nervous of being rebellious and not following the pattern writers' every direction, but in our opinion, they needn't be. It's true that we have all had some shockers in our time, such as choosing a completely inappropriate yarn for a project with disastrous results. We could have seen these experiences as a complete waste of our time and energy, but being optimists (at least when it comes to knitting) and people always eager to learn from our mistakes, we would either unravel the yarn for another use or hide it in the darkest corner of our wardrobes and move on. Nobody's perfect, are they? The more experienced we got, however, the more we realised there were a few simple tricks that can be employed to minimise damaging the design of the pattern while introducing a new yarn to it, and we will share them with you here:

- It is imperative to use a substitute yarn that has the same tension as that for which the pattern was designed (check the yarn label for this).
- Always, and we mean always, do a tension square before diving straight into a pattern (we'll get to the ins and out of tension squares in a little bit). This is true even if you are using the suggested yarn. Apart from making sure the sizing will be correct given your personal tension, you should get a good idea of what the yarn looks like when knitted up and be able to judge whether it's likely to work for the project at hand. If you're still umming and ahhing about it, do a larger sample – it'll save you loads of time in the long run, we promise. If you're substituting a yarn it's essential you use one with the same tension as the one suggested in the pattern.
- It's generally advisable to use a yarn with similar fibre content to the

one stated in the pattern, if possible. Patterns are carefully designed to work with the drape, texture and other characteristics of a specific yarn, so if you want a similar result, try to find a comparable yarn. On the other hand, we wouldn't stick hard and fast to this rule.

Yes, you might not get a result like the pretty picture on the pattern, but you might have discovered a totally unique look that puts the designed pattern to shame! Go on, we dare you.

- Try your best to use a yarn with the same metreage as the one suggested in the pattern. Although yarns are usefully categorised into different 'weights' (as described earlier in this chapter), yarns in the same category can vary, so it's always best to match the metreage of the yarn suggested to the substitute yarn, rather than just go by the weight.

GRANNY'S
PURL OF WISDOM

If you're having trouble finding a yarn that you like, you could always combine two or more strands of thinner yarn to create a single thicker one. These can even be strands of differing colours that you can blend to create your very own marled yarn!

Use this cunning equation to check how many strands of the thinner yarn you'll need to make up the thicker one:

$$\frac{\text{Thicker Yarn Weight}}{\text{Thinner Yarn Weight}} \times \frac{\text{Thicker Yarn Meterage}}{\text{Thinner Yarn Metreage}} = \frac{\text{No. of Strands}}{\text{Required}}$$

For a perfect match you're ideally looking for a round number, but rounding up or down by 0.2m should be negligible. Anything more than that, though, and you should really choose another yarn.

All the Gear and No Idea

Unless you're about to launch into a bit of finger knitting (a whole other book entirely), you're going to need to know a little about knitting needles before you get started.

Now, back in our day needles were mainly made out of steel, but nowadays they seem to be available in all kinds of materials, including aluminium, bamboo, wood, plastic and glass. It's totally down to personal preference which will suit you best, so nip down to your local yarn store and try holding a few different types to get a feel for the various textures. Our particular favourite over at Grannies, Inc. are bamboo needles, as they are light and smooth to hold and actually warm up as you knit (as do most needles made from natural materials).
There are three types of needle out there...

Straight Needles

These are the most common type of needle and are used in pairs. Knitting is almost always depicted on television and in movies using straight needles, so we're certain you will have an idea of what we're talking about here. They look like a stick with one tapered end that is used to work the stitches and a knob on the other end to make sure the stitches don't fall off. Straight needles are used for flat knitting, where the fabric is produced by knitting a row of stitches from one needle to the other, turning and knitting a row of stitches back onto the first needle, continuing back and forth.

Double-Pointed Needles

Although not the most common, double-pointed knitting needles are the oldest type of needle and, as the name suggests, taper to a point at both ends, allowing them to be knit from either end. They are generally

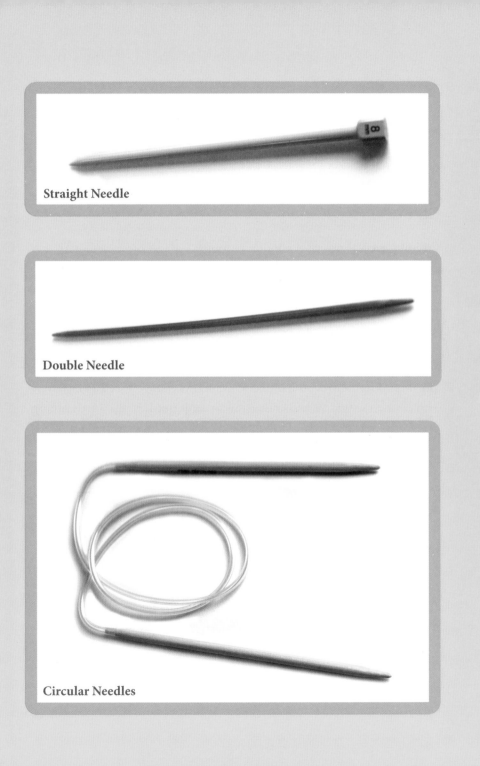

Straight Needle

Double Needle

Circular Needles

sold in packs of four or five and are used mainly for circular knitting (see page 64), where you knit continuously in a spiral to produce a tube of fabric. However, ever since some clever bod invented the circular needle, double-pointed needles have become somewhat redundant, although they are still really useful for knitting small, tubular pieces such as socks and sleeves. Of course, some knitters just simply prefer them.

Circular Needles

Circular needles are very popular amongst us Grannies, Inc. lot as they can be used for both circular (see page 64) and flat knitting. They consist of two needles tapered at one end and joined at the other end by a flexible cord. For flat knitting the stitches are worked from one needle to the other, turned, then knitted back in exactly the same way as with straight needles except the stitches are allowed to fall off the back end of the needle as they are caught by the cord. This is very useful when knitting wider fabrics, as a longer cord allows many more stitches to be held than would be possible using straight needles. It's worth noting that using circular needles to knit flat is not everyone's cup of tea, so try out both straight and circulars and see which work best for you.

When using them to knit in the round the same principal is used as when working with double-pointed needles and the stitches are knit continuously in a spiral.

Needle Length

Although straight knitting needles used to only be available in a few different lengths, manufacturers are now making a wider selection to choose from. The length of the needle determines how many stitches you can fit onto it and hence the width of the fabric you can achieve. If faced with having to choose between two needle lengths we'd always go for the longer, just because it maximises their use; however, some knitters prefer to match the needles to each project. Many patterns won't specify the length of needle required so it is mainly a case of using your common sense. If you are buying needles for a specific design that only involves knitting narrow pieces of fabric, you're likely to be more comfortable with shorter needles.

When buying circular knitting needles you must also decide which cord length to choose. If you're buying them for flat knitting the cord length doesn't really matter, but if you're buying them for circular knitting the larger the circumference of the piece you are looking to knit, the longer the cord you will need. If you try to knit a circular piece with a small circumference using needles with a very long cord you will wind up endlessly shuffling the stitches around the cord, so it's recommended you try to match the cord length to the circumference as closely as possible.

If you're a fan of circular needles it may be worth investing in a whole kit that offers a range of needle sizes with detachable ends and a number of different-length cords that can be attached to them to create any combination you require. They are fairly pricey, though – maybe one for the Christmas list?

Needle Size (Width)

The diameter of your needles determines the size of the stitches they produce. In general, the thicker the yarn the larger the recommended needle size, however, the combination of yarn weight and needle size is what really determines the outcome of the resulting fabric. For instance, thinner yarns knit on larger needles will create a more open, lacy fabric, while thicker yarns knit on smaller needles will create a tight, more rigid fabric.

There are three widely used knitting needle size systems, which can be hugely confusing when reading patterns. We've put together the handy little conversion chart (right) to help you decipher the sizing when you come across it in patterns and so you can be sure you choose the right-sized needles to get started with your project.

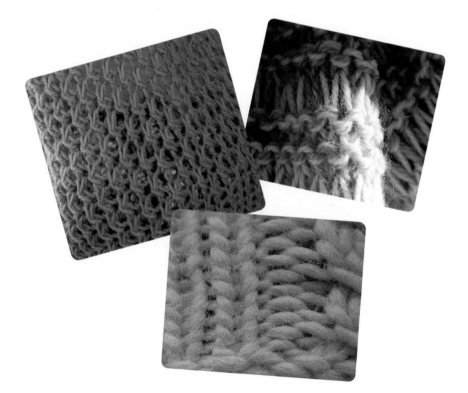

Needle Size Conversion Chart

Metric (mm)	UK	US
2	14	0
2.25	13	1
2.75	12	2
3	11	
3.25	10	3
3.5		4
3.75	9	5
4	8	6
4.5	7	7
5	6	8
5.5	5	9
6	4	10
6.5	3	10½
7	2	
7.5	1	
8	0	11
9	00	13
10	000	15
12		17
16		19
19		35
25		50

Other Bits and Bob(bin)s

If you've got yourself some yarn and needles you're pretty much ready to get cracking, but there are other little bits and bobs that are useful to have in your box, too, so that when a pattern calls for something specific you'll have it to hand. You can look out for these bits in the shops and pick them up as and when you need them, or if you prefer you can commit to the knit and gather them all up ready from the start.

- **Ruler and/or tape measure** You'll need these to measure your tension squares and for the length of your work because some patterns ask you to work a certain number of centimetres rather than state the number of rows.
- **Scissors** Nothing big, just a small, sharp-pointed pair of scissors for cutting yarn.
- **A needle gauge** This is a really useful piece of kit for measuring the size of your needles. Not all needles are marked with their size so how are you going to know how big they are otherwise? Just pop the needle through each of the holes in the gauge until you find a hole that fits just right.
- **Stitch markers** These are little coloured rings that are slipped onto your needle at a position at which you need to remember to do something – such as increase or decrease – in a pattern. Stitch markers allow you to empty your mind while knitting but give you the little jolt you need when you should be paying attention.
- **Stitch holders** Certain patterns call for you to slip some stitches off the needles for a time, so to save them unravelling and you pulling your hair out, a stitch holder can be used to hold these stitches until they are safely back on the needles.
- **Safety pins** Always good to have around, these pins can be used as stitch markers, stitch holders or to hold together pieces of work when sewing the seams together.
- **Row counters** Being as forgetful as we are it's hard to keep track of

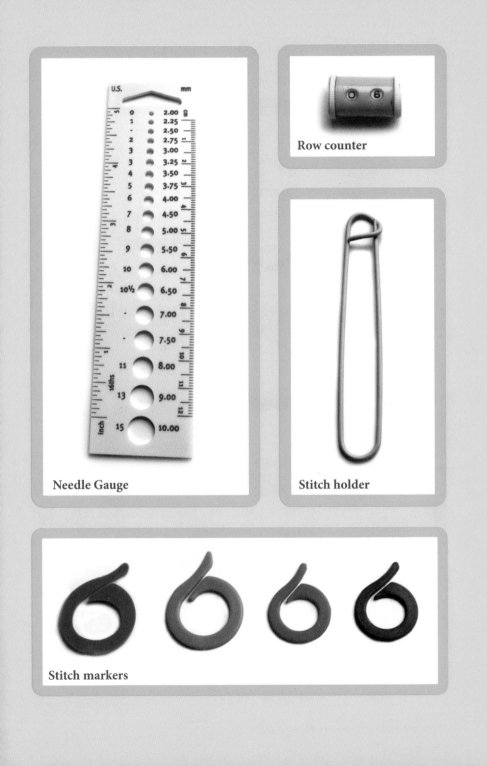

Needle Gauge

Row counter

Stitch holder

Stitch markers

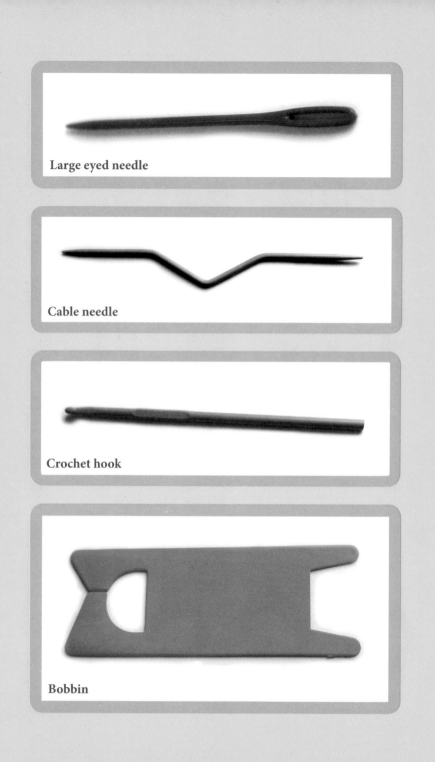

Large eyed needle

Cable needle

Crochet hook

Bobbin

how many rows we have knitted. This is where the wonderful row counter comes in. It simply slips onto one needle and as you knit each row you increase it by one – magic!

- **Large-eyed yarn needle** This is needed for darning in all those pesky yarn ends you're left with after finishing knitting your project and for sewing up seams.
- **Cable needles** Once you're up and running you're most likely to want to try out the amazing cable stitch and might be thinking, 'how on earth do I create that twist in the pattern?' Well, we won't go into all the detail now, but get yourself a cable needle in readiness as you won't be able to try them without one!
- **Bobbins** These are small, funny looking things that have a hole in one end and a two prongs coming out of the other. They are used for holding a length of yarn when working on intarsia to prevent the different-coloured strands of yarn getting tangled up at the back of your work.
- **Crochet hook** Crocheting is a totally different kettle of fish from knitting, but the good old crochet hook can come in very handy when you've made a mistake in your knitting and you need to hunt down a stray loop and hook it back into place. Nobody's perfect, so don't sweat it and get out your hook.
- **Graph paper** This patterned paper is really useful when you want to create a visual picture of knitting instructions in a pattern or create your own charts for intarsia or Fair Isle knitting. Count each little square as a stitch and shade or mark them according to the pattern.

How to Read a Knitting Pattern

Tension (or Gauge)

Tension is one of the most important measures to take to ensure the success of a project. Tension is the number of stitches and rows you will get per centimetre of fabric given a particular needle size and yarn. It is a very personal measurement as every knitter creates a slightly different tension as they knit; some knit very tightly, some very loosely. It is therefore imperative that you check your tension before launching into a project, otherwise you're likely to find all of your hard work has gone to waste when the sizing of your finished garment is wrong. Every good pattern should have a tension at the beginning – this will have come from the designer who wrote it, usually telling you how many stitches and rows they achieve to a 10cm square using a particular stitch. You'll need to knit a tension square (commonly known as a swatch) in the suggested needle size and yarn (or substitute yarn) and adjust the needle size if your tension does not match that of the designer.

HOW TO KNIT A TENSION SQUARE

- Using the stitch stated in the pattern's tension detail, knit a piece of fabric 15cm or so square and cast off loosely.
- Follow the finishing instructions in the pattern and block or steam the square on a flat surface.
- Place a pin halfway up the square a 1cm or so in from the left edge, perpendicular to the cast-on edge. Lay a ruler flat on the square parallel to the cast-on edge so that the point of the pin touches the 0cm mark.
- Place a second pin parallel to the first at the 10cm mark on the ruler.
- Turn the square 90° and repeat the previous two bullet points.

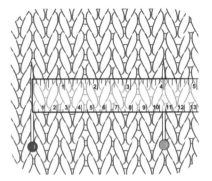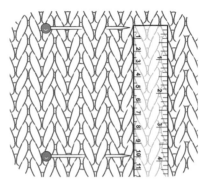

- Count the number of stitches and the number of rows between the pins and you will have your tension.

You'll now need to compare your tension with the one in the pattern. If your tension has too few stitches you need to go down a needle size; if it has too many stitches you need to go up a needle size. If you have had to go up or down a needle size you need to start all over again and do another tension square using the adjusted needle size and repeat until your tension matches the one in the pattern.

Abbreviations

Knitting patterns would be extremely long and confusing if they were written out in full, so they are nearly always abbreviated. Phew! At first, trying to read a pattern can seem very daunting, but once you know the lingo you'll find that most are really very easy to interpret. Below are the most frequently used abbreviations, grouped by what they describe. Anything more specific should be explained in the patterns themselves.

Type of stitch	Insertion point of stitch	Overall pattern
st(s) = stitch(es) k = knit p = purl sl = slip yo = yarn over	k-b/k1b = knit into row below p-b/p1b = purl into row below	* = repeat instructions following * * = repeat instructions between ( ) = work instructions between st st = stockingette stitch rev st st = reverse stockingette stitch g st = garter stitch
Scope of stitch tog = together psso = pass slipped stitch over pnso = pass next stitch over	**Short combinations of stitches** MB = make bobble ssk = slip, slip, knit skp = slip, knit, pass	
		Increases & decreases m1 = make one stitch by picking up loop between stitch just worked and next and working into the back kfb/inc 1 = increase by knitting into front and back of stitch pfb = increase by purling into front and back of stitch inc = increas(e)(ing) dec = decreas(e)(ing)
Orientation of stitch tbl = through back of loop(s) kwise = knitwise pwise = purlwise	**Repetition of stitches** alt = alternate rep = repeat(ing)
Lengths & weights cm = centimetre(s) in = inch(es) mm = millimetre(s) g = gram(mes) oz = ounce(s)	**Position of yarn** wyib/yb = with yarn in back wyif/yf(wd) = with yarn in front yon = yarn over needle yrn = yarn round needle yrfr = yarn forward round needle	
		Positional abbreviations rem = remain(ing) foll = follow(ing) beg = begin(ning) cont = continu(e)(ing) incl = includ(e)(ing)
Beginnings and endings CO = cast on BO = bind off / cast off	**Side of work** RS = right side WS = wrong side	**Colour changes** A, B, C, D = contrasting colours

Commit to the Knit

LET'S GET THIS PARTY STARTED

First Things First –
How to Look Good Knitting

Everybody has a different style when it comes to knitting. Whichever way you hold your needles and yarn it is going to feel a bit awkward for a while until you get used to it, a bit like holding a golf club. As you already know, we're fans of individualism and don't want to tell you to hold your needles and yarn one way or the other, it should be what is most comfortable for you. So try out a few different styles and find the one that gets your groove on.

How to Hold Your Needles

There are generally two ways in which you can do this:

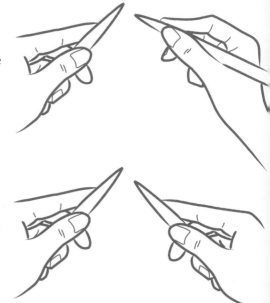

1. Hold the left needle as you would a fork (or knife, for you lefties out there) and the right needle as you would a pencil.

2. Hold the left and right needles as you would a knife and fork.

Get Your Style On

There are two different styles of knitting, and which one you choose will determine in which hand you hold your yarn. If you knit 'English' style you hold the yarn in your right hand; if you knit 'Continental' style you have the yarn in your left hand. There is no right way or wrong way, you are just looking for the method that suits you and gives you a nice, even tension throughout your knitting. We recommend that lefties try the Continental style first before trying 'backwards knitting', which involves following knitting instructions in mirror reverse, because this means you can read patterns the way they were written, along with the righties.

> ### GRANNY'S
> ### PURL OF WISDOM
>
> With all this new technology around there are loads more ways to learn to knit than back in our day. If you're ever stuck on a particular stitch or knitting instruction – 'Google it'! You'll find all kinds of videos, blogs and illustrations to help you get to grips with even the most confusing of techniques.

THE ENGLISH STYLE

This is the traditional and most common style of knitting. The yarn is held in the right hand and wrapped around the right needle before being pulled through to create the stitch. The English style is kinder to the less-coordinated knitter because it requires less precision to accomplish a stitch, so we'd recommend this technique to children or uncoordinated adults in particular.

Some people like to let go of the right-hand needle in order to wrap the yarn, while others like to keep the yarn close to the top of their index finger and to the needle point so that they just need to lift their index finger to wrap the yarn, creating a more fluid knitting motion. Which way will you do it, we wonder?

THE CONTINENTAL STYLE

On the Continent (or any continent for that matter) there is a new breed of knitter, kicking back and quietly revolting against the English. They like to be all cool and trendy with their new knitting ways and we say – hoorah! The more knitters out there the better, so if they want to be all different and non-conformist let them. We embrace you.

The Continental style involves holding the yarn in the left hand, allowing the knitter to scoop up the yarn with the right needle and pulling it through to make a stitch.

Although we consider ourselves traditionalists, we've got to admit this method is rather inviting and a few of our lot have even admitted to converting to the Continental method of late. It's incredibly efficient when changing frequently from knit to purl stitches, making rib and moss stitch seem like a doddle. The Continental style is rumoured to be the faster of the two methods but we'd challenge anyone to a race any day. Needles at the ready, yarn steady, let's goooooo.

(Note that in the majority of this book we teach using the English style so as not to have to explain everything twice. It should be easy peasy, lemon squeezy to adapt everything to the Continental method – simply swap the hand from which the yarn is fed).

How to Hold Your Yarn

No matter which style floats your boat and which hand you choose to hold your yarn, you'll still need to feed the yarn in a way that allows it to pass through your fingers smoothly and create an even tension.

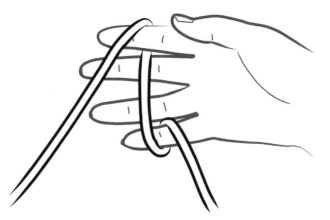

The way you wind the yarn in, out and around your fingers is completely up to whatever feels right to you, but here is the method we most commonly use, just in case you were wondering...

Start by holding out your hand with your fingers pointing left (right hand) or right (left hand), palms facing. Starting with the yarn in front, feed the yarn over and around your little finger, bringing the yarn back to the front and creating a loop.

Now lay the yarn across your ring and middle fingers vertically, through the gap between your index and middle fingers and round the tip of your index finger. The yarn should now flow smoothly through your fingers as your index finger wraps the yarn around the needle to create a stitch.

Casting on

The very first step in any hand-knitting project is pulling up a comfy chair, turning on the radio or TV and pouring yourself a nice cup of tea. Once settled, it's the cast on.

Casting on is simply the technique by which you get the first stitches onto a needle from which you start knitting. There are lots of different ways to cast on, so if you are already comfortable with one method we recommend you don't change it. Each method results in tighter or looser edges, so try casting on and knitting a small swatch using a few different ones so you can see the difference for yourself.

Slip Knot (and we don't mean the heavy metal American band)

Most cast-on methods begin with a slip knot – which turns out to be rather easier to do than to actually explain! Try following these steps over and over again and before you know it you'll be making slip knots in seconds.

1. Hold your left index and middle finger together in front of you, palms facing, as if you are about to play at shooting someone. Let the yarn hang from these fingers with a tail at least 15cm falling in front and the rest of the ball falling behind.
2. Using your right hand, reach round from behind to wrap the tail clockwise around the yarn that is hanging at the back and hold it loosely to the right-hand side, creating a large loop over two fingers.
3. Open your two fingers slightly and hang the tail from front to back over the bottom one to create a small loop over one finger.
4. Clamp your fingers closed again and pull the larger loop over the small loop and off your fingers. Pull the yarn from the ball tightly to create a knot below. Slip the remaining loop onto a needle and pull the tail tightly to create your first stitch.

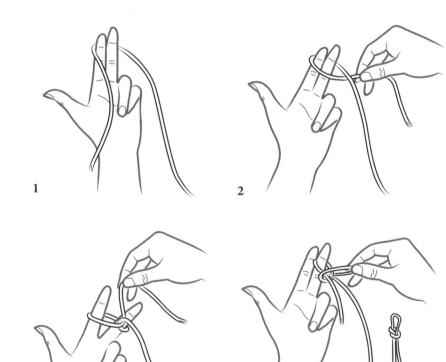

1

2

3

4

Knit Cast On

As its name suggests, this method involves casting on using a series of knit stitches, so if you learn this one it's a bonus because you'll be learning the knit stitch as well. It's not too hard to do and is a good choice for most projects as it's relatively stretchy and versatile.

GRANNY'S PURL OF WISDOM

If your pattern asks you to 'cast on loosely', try casting on using a slightly larger needle, then revert back to the right-sized needle when you start your first row. It'll save you trying to guess how much slack to give the yarn on each cast-on stitch and will give you an even but loose edge.

1. Insert the right-hand needle into your first stitch (slip knot) from front to back, left to right. Place the left-hand needle into the stitch too, right to left.
2. Wrap the yarn clockwise around the tip of the right-hand needle.
3. Pull the right-hand needle back through the first stitch, bringing with it the new loop.
4. Insert the left-hand needle into the front of the new loop from right to left and slip it off the right-hand needle. Pull the yarn so that the loop is secure but not too tight, as that will make it hard to knit your first row. Repeat until you have the required number of cast-on stitches on your left-hand needle.

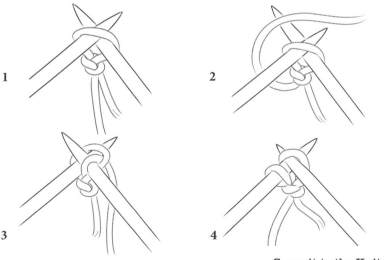

1

2

3

4

Cable Cast On

Unlike the knit cast on, the cable cast on won't help you master the cable stitch, it just vaguely resembles a cable if you look at it closely. (Unlucky!) This method creates a firm edge that doesn't stretch, so it's best not to use it for sleeves or other openings where you might want a bit of give.

Begin the cable cast on in the same way as you would for the knit cast on, until you have completed step 4. Then follow these instructions:

5. Insert the right-hand needle between the last two stitches on the left-hand needle.
6. Continue as you did with the second stitch, wrapping the yarn clockwise around the tip of the needle and pull the loop back between the two stitches.
7. Insert the left-hand needle into the front of the new loop from right to left, slip it off the right-hand needle, then pull to secure.
8. Repeat until you have the required number of cast-on stitches on your left-hand needle.

5

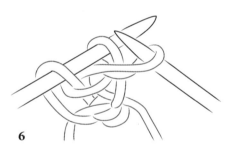

6

7

Wrap Cast On

This is easy peasy and very fast once you get going, so it's a great one to enable beginners to get stitches on their needles and get started with the harder stuff. It's the only method we know that doesn't require a slip knot, so if you were baffled by those this is you best bet; the technique gives a fairly stretchy edge, so it's great for jumpers. You'll only need one needle to do a wrap cast on.

Hold your needle in your right hand and with your index finger hold the yarn in place against the needle, leaving a 10cm or so tail hanging down to the right.

1. Using the thumb and middle finger of your left hand, pinch the yarn coming off the needle towards the ball a little way away from the needle (the distance required will become clear once you try casting on a few stitches).
2. Lift up the yarn between the needle and the pinch using your left index finger, then rotate your left hand so that you are pointing your index finger directly away from you. The yarn should cross, just creating a loop hanging over your index finger.

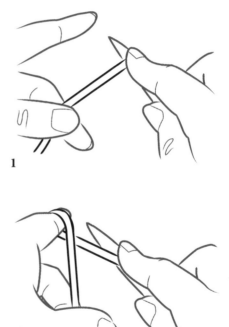

1

2

3. Take the point of the needle and push it through this loop from front to back, slipping your finger off in the process. Hey presto – you have your first stitch!
4. Repeat these steps a few more times to make sure the tail is secure. Then let the tail drop and continue scooping up more stitches to your heart's content.

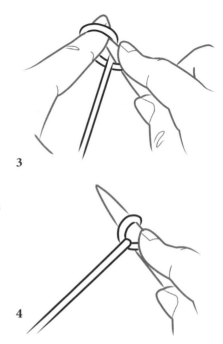

Knit One

Now you've got all those stitches cast on, it's time to get on and teach you your very first stitch. The knit stitch is classic, timeless, and is the one to know. It will feel awkward to begin with but you mark our words, with a bit of practice this stitch will become second nature to you and before you know it you'll be doing it without even looking. Just follow these five easy steps for each stitch on your left needle to complete a row, switch the right needle (now holding all the stitches) into your left hand and start all over again.

Hold your needles however they feel comfortable (see page 46), with the stitches on the needle in your left hand and the yarn feeding through your right hand behind the right needle (English style – reverse for Continental style).

1. Insert the point of your right needle into the first stitch on the left-hand needle, working front to back, left to right.
2. Using your index finger, wrap the yarn around the point of the right needle, anti-clockwise.
3. Holding the yarn taut, bring the point of the right needle back through the stitch (the way it went in), bringing the loop with it so that it is now in front of the left needle. Slide the needle point up through it a little way to make sure the loop doesn't fall off the needle.Slide the stitch off by moving the right needle along and off the point of the left needle. You should be left with a new stitch (the loop) on the right needle and the knitted stitch below it.

GRANNY'S
PURL OF WISDOM

It's really useful to be able to know the difference in the appearance of the knit and purl stitches so that you can recognise each of them. Often patterns will require you to work a stitch according to whether the one below is a knit or purl stitch, so take a close look at both and familiarise yourself with which is which.

Knit
stitch

Purl
stitch

A knit stitch looks exactly the same as a purl stitch from behind and vice versa, so if you knit one row and turn you will be looking at a row of purl stitches.

Purl One

The second-best stitch to know is the purl stitch, which is as easy as the knit stitch once you know how. With a combination of knit and purl stitches the world is your oyster, so get this one under your belt now and there'll be no stopping you!

Hold your needles however they feel comfortable (see page 46), with the stitches on the needle in your left hand and the yarn feeding through your right hand in front of the right needle (English style – reverse for Continental style).

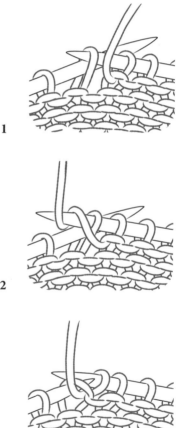

1. Insert the point of your right needle into the first stitch on the left-hand needle in the opposite way to the knit stitch: working back to front, right to left.
2. Using your index finger, wrap the yarn around the point of the right needle, anti-clockwise.
3. Holding the yarn taut, bring the point of the right needle back through the stitch (the way it went in), taking the loop with it so that it is now behind the left needle. Slide the needle point up through it a little way to make sure the loop doesn't fall off the needle. Slide the stitch off by moving the right needle along and off the point of the left needle. You should be left with a new stitch (the loop) on the right needle and the original stitch below it.

1

2

3

Casting off (or Binding off)

If you've reached the casting off stage then may we say 'congratulations'? This must mean that you've come to the end of your first piece of knitting – even if it is only a few experimental rows! Americans call this process binding off, but we British grannies like to call it casting off; either way, it's really easy, so don't sweat it. Casting off is simply getting the stitches off the needle in a way that means they won't unravel (don't even try just pulling the needle out)!

   Below we'll describe how to cast off knitwise, which is perfect for casting off stocking stitch; however, you should always cast off 'in pattern'. For example, if you have been working in a 2 x 2 rib pattern you should cast off the two knit stitches knitwise, followed by the two purl stitches purlwise (purl the stitches on the left needle rather than knit them).

1. At the beginning of your cast-off row, knit two stitches as normal.
2. Now, take your left needle point and push it through the front of the first stitch on the right needle.
3. Using the left needle, lift this stitch over the top of the second stitch and let it drop off the end of the right needle.

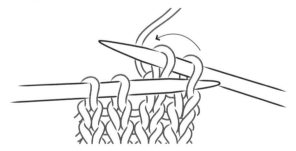

4. Knit one more stitch as normal.
5. Repeat steps 2–4 until you have knit all the stitches on the left needle.
6. Cut the yarn, leaving a 15cm or so tail, slip the final stitch off the needle and feed the tail through the loop, pulling gently.

5 Stitches Everyone Should Know (Young'un to Granny)

Garter Stitch

Possibly the easiest stitch out there, garter stitch consists of row after row of knitted stitches. It creates a chunky, bumpy fabric that looks the same on either side and stretches easily in one direction.

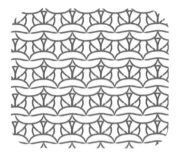

Row 1: K all sts.
Repeat row 1 throughout.

Stocking Stitch
(known as Stockinette Stitch across the pond)

By far the most common stitch, you'll have seen this stitch around all over the place. Stocking stitch is made up of one row of knitted stitches followed by one row of purled stitches repeated over and over again. The resulting fabric is as smooth as a baby's bottom on one side (the 'right side') and bumpy as a herd of camels on the other (the 'wrong side').

Row 1: K all sts.
Row 2: P all sts.
Repeat rows 1–2 throughout.

If you're after reverse stocking stitch, simply start with the purl row so that the bumpy side becomes the 'right side'.

Rib Stitch

This is another common stitch that you've probably seen at the bottom of your jumpers and the top of your socks. Rib stitch creates a stripy looking fabric that stretches a great deal when pulled from either side. This makes it perfect for openings in garments that need to stretch when being pulled on but retract once in place.

The stitch is made up of a two-row pattern, with the first row consisting of one or more knit stitches followed by one or more purl stitches, repeated. You must move the yarn between the two needles mid-row when changing between knit and purl stitches in order to position it at the front or back as required. On the second row you must knit the knit stitches (those that you purled on the first row) and purl the purl stitches (those that you knitted on the first row) to create vertical bars of alternating stitches.

GRANNY'S PURL OF WISDOM

Stocking stitch fabric has a horrid tendency to curl at the edges, so if you're planning on knitting a flat item like a scarf using this stitch, try knitting 3–5 stitches of another stitch, such as garter or moss at the start and end of each row. This will give you a pretty border along the sides of your piece and means you won't end up with one big tube of knitted fabric!

Ribs are named according to the number of knit and purl stitches that make up their pattern. To make an even rib for a flat item you should cast on a multiple of the stitches in the rib pattern plus an additional set of the knit stitches. For example, in the case of a 2 x 4 rib you'll need 8, 14, 20, 26, etc. stitches.

1 x 1 Rib -   Row 1: *K1, P1, rep from * to last st. K1.
                   Row 2: P1. *K1, P1, rep from * to end.
2 x 2 Rib -   Row 1: *K2, P2, rep from * to last st. K2.
                   Row 2: P2. *K2, P2, rep from * to end.

2 x 4 Rib - Row 1: *K2, P4, rep from * to last st. K2
Row 2: P2. *K4, P2, rep from * to end.
All: Repeat rows 1–2 throughout.

If you're knitting a circular piece flat, to create a seamless join to your rib you should make sure you're working with exactly a multiple of the stitches in the rib pattern. For example, in the case of a 2 x 4 rib you'll need 6, 12, 18, 24, etc. stitches.

2 x 4 Rib - Row 1: *K2, P4, rep from * to end.
Row 2: *K4, P2, rep from * to end.
Repeat rows 1–2 throughout.

Moss Stitch
(known as Seed Stitch across the pond)

Moss stitch is one of our favourites, as it gives a most luscious texture of tiny bobbles all over its fabric. It's not usually used for any specific purpose and is mainly decorative. The stitch is reversible so it doesn't really have a 'right side' and a 'wrong side', making it good for flat items such as blankets and scarves. Moss stitch is identical to 1 x 1 rib in its first row. You know all about 1 x 1 rib already, so what are you waiting for? Get that first row done! For the second row you must now knit the purl stitches and purl the knit stitches. However, the pattern changes depending on whether you are working an odd or an even number of stitches...

Odd number of stitches - Row 1: *K1, P1, rep from * to last st. K1.
Row 2: K1. *P1, K1, rep from * to end.
Even number of stitches - Row 1: *K1, P1, rep from * to end.
Row 2: *P1, K1, rep from * to end.
All Repeat rows 1–2 throughout.

Cable Stitch

You've probably come across cables running through various jumpers, cardies and scarves, and now that you're teetering on the edge of becoming a confirmed knitter you're likely to be thinking, 'how on earth do I go about knitting them?' They look so beautifully decorative twisting and knotting their way up a pair of socks or cricket jumper

that you are bound to want to try them out sooner rather than later, so we're here to tell you not to be afraid, they are not going to bite (unless you hang them over a crocodile).

Cable knitting involves crossing two sets of stitches to create a twist in the fabric. Simply transfer the first half of the cable stitches onto a cable needle (hold it in front if you want a twist to the left and behind if you want a twist to the right), knit the second half of the cable stitches as normal, then knit the first half, either by transferring them back onto the left needle or by knitting them straight off the cable needle. You should end up with the two halves crossing over each other, which, when you do this 'turning' row every 4–10 rows, creates a rope-like feature through the fabric. The fewer rows between turning rows, the tighter the resulting knot.

Patterns involving cables should provide you with what's called a 'cable panel', which describes each stitch and row in the cable segment of the overall pattern. Below are a couple of cable instructions you might see in these panels, and an explanation of what you should do when you come across them...

C4F (CABLE FOUR FRONT)

1. Slip the next two stitches on the left needle onto a cable needle and hold it in front.
2. Knit the next two stitches as normal.
3. Either slip the two stitches from the cable needle back onto the left needle and knit them, or knit them directly from the cable needle.

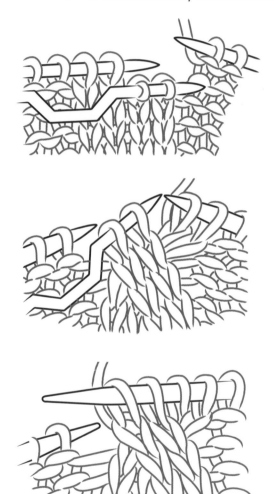

1

2

3

C4B (CABLE FOUR BEHIND)

1. Slip the next two stitches on the left needle onto a cable needle and hold it behind.
2. Knit the next two stitches as normal.
3. Either slip the two stitches from the cable needle back onto the left needle and knit them, or knit them directly from the cable needle.

As you might have already cleverly deciphered, a cable instruction will consist of a 'C' (telling the knitter this is a cable) followed by a number (the number of stitches involved in the cable) and either an 'F' or a 'B' (indicating whether the knitter should hold the stitches in front or behind the work).

A standard cable instruction will involve an even number of stitches (with equal halves crossing each other) and will have the same number of rows between turning rows as the number of stitches involved in the cable.

Circular knitting

We are a big fan of circular knitting here at Grannies, Inc., as it is a fabulous way of knitting beanies – which is where we started. Circular knitting requires special needles that enable you to join your first stitch to your last so that you don't have to turn at the end of each row and can continue knitting round and round, creating a tube of fabric. For this reason, when you knit circularly each row of knitting is called a 'round' and you are often referred to as 'knitting in the round'. For anything tubular within a pattern we certainly recommend using circular knitting as it avoids any sewing up or seaming.

There are two types of needle available for circular knitting; they give the same result but do require a slightly different technique.

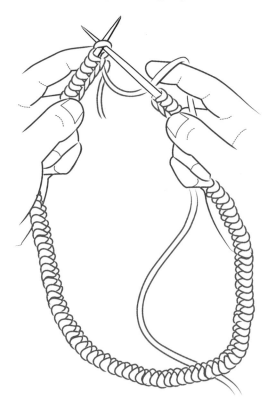

Circular Needles

Circular needles look like two regular needles joined together at one end by a wire or cord (see page 31). The needles come in all the regular widths and the wire in a number of different lengths. Ideally, you want the needle length to be smaller than the circumference of the tube you are trying to knit in order to create a smooth and continual knitting motion, otherwise you'll find yourself constantly pushing and pulling the stitches around the wire and are likely to end up with an uneven tension.

To knit on circular needles, begin by casting on the required number of stitches and spreading them evenly over the needles and wire. Hold the needles together so that the first cast-on stitch is on the left needle, the last on the right needle and none of the stitches are twisted (the bottom of each cast-on stitch should be facing inwards). Knit the first stitch on the left needle to join all of the stitches in the round and pull the yarn tightly to avoid any gap. Continue to knit stitches off the left needle onto the right and just keep on spiralling upwards into a tube.

> ### GRANNY'S
> ## PURL OF WISDOM
>
> The only downside to a seamless piece of knitting is the fact that you can get quite lost as to where you are in each round. Try placing a stitch marker on the needle before joining the first round and slipping it every round so you always know where one round ends and the next begins.

Double-pointed needles

Cleverly named, double-pointed needles (see page 31) have a point at both ends. Ta-daaa! These needles are usually sold in packs of four or five. Having four is sufficient to be able to knit in the round, but opt for five if possible so you have a spare. You'll need to use double-pointers when there are too few stitches to comfortably fit on your circular needles, such as for small tubular items (socks, gloves, etc.). While double-pointed needles can seem intimidating at first, our advice is to stay calm and don't panic – they're not all that bad, really! We will tell you now they will be very uncomfortable to hold to begin with, very awkward indeed, but as you practise they will start to feel like second nature and you'll soon have socks coming out of your ears!

To knit on double-pointed needles, first cast on the required number of stitches onto a single needle and then divide them equally between three needles so that you end up with a triangle of stitches. This triangle will have one open end between the first and last cast-on stitches. With the first cast-on stitch on the left needle, hold the triangle with the open end pointing towards you and make sure that none of the stitches are twisted (the bottom of each cast-on stitch should be facing downwards). Using your spare, 'free' needle, knit the first titch on the left needle to join all of the stitches in the round and pull the yarn tightly to avoid any gap. Continue to knit all of the stitches off the left needle; when done, this will become your 'free' needle. Pick up the second needle in the triangle in your left hand and, using the free needle, knit all stitches on the left needle as you did the first. Repeat this action for the last needle in the triangle and you will have completed one round. Do it over and over again and you will start to see a tube forming and, hey presto, you're now a double-pointed knitter!

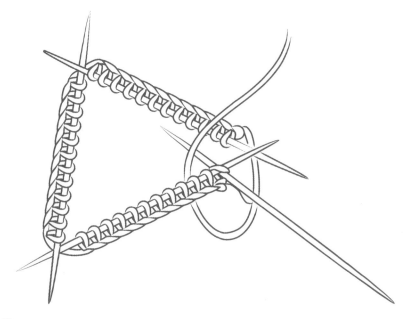

Basic Shaping

Even though scarves and blankets are really fun to knit, you'll be limited to producing only rectangular items if you don't learn to 'shape' your knitting. It's very common for patterns to include some basic shaping techniques, which involve increasing and decreasing stitches. Increasing will widen the fabric and decreasing will narrow the fabric, and it is often the case that shaping will happen evenly across a row to create a symmetrical result.

Increasing

There are two common methods of increasing stitches along a row of knitting: knitting into the front and back of a stitch to create two stitches out of one, or picking up and knitting the strand of yarn lying between two stitches to create an extra stitch. The latter increase should appear relatively invisible on stocking stitch fabric and so too the former on textured fabric, such as moss stitch, but for decorative reasons this might not be a bonus and you might want to switch them around.

KFB/INC 1 (KNIT INTO FRONT AND BACK/ INCREASE BY ONE)

1. Go ahead and knit the first stitch on your left needle but stop before you slide it off the needle.
2. Move your right needle behind the left and knit again into the back of the same stitch, this time sliding the stitch off the left needle to create two new stitches on the right needle.

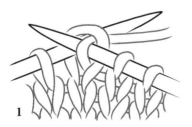

You can achieve this increase on the purl side of your knitting by purling into the front and back of the same stitch (PFB). Let us warn you now that it can be fiddly trying to purl into the back of the stitch but be patient, take it slowly and you'll get it in the end.

M1 (MAKE ONE)

In 'making' one stitch you create a twist in the new stitch to avoid leaving a hole underneath the increase. This twist can either turn to the left or to the right.

To twist to the left:
1. Pick up the strand running between the last stitch you worked and the next stitch by inserting the left needle under the strand from front to back to create a new loop.
2. Knit into the back of this loop.

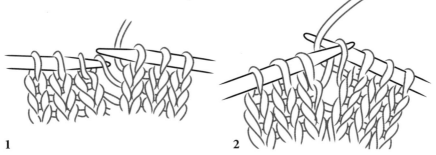

1   2

To twist to the right:
1. Pick up the strand running between the last stitch you worked and the next stitch by inserting the left needle under the strand from back to front to create a new loop.
2. Knit into the front of this loop.

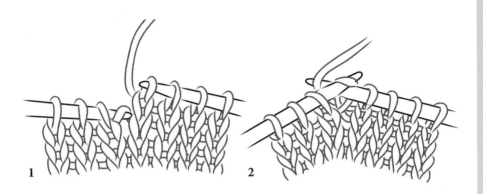

1   2

THE YARNOVER (YO)

A less common way to increase stitches is by using the yarnover technique. Yarnovers create holes in the fabric and hence are usually accompanied by a decrease stitch to produce lacy effects, rather than to widen a piece of knitwear.

  YO is a generic (and US) term indicating that the yarn needs to be wound around the right needle to create a new loop, which becomes the new stitch. The yarnover consists of three easy steps:

1. Prepare for the yarn over: If the yarn is not already in the front of your work, bring it between the two needles so that it is.
2. Yarnover: Take the yarn over the right-hand needle from the front to the back.

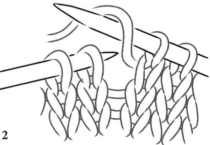

1   2

3. Prepare for the next stitch: If the next stitch is a purl stitch, bring the yarn between the two needles so that it is at the front ready to purl. (If it is a knit stitch, the yarn will already be in the correct position at the back.)

On the return row you'll need to knit or purl the yarnovers according to the pattern to turn them into stitches of their very own and, hey presto, you will have increased the width of your work.

Quite confusingly, we Brits use a number of different terms that relate to the combination of steps needed to achieve a yarnover between differing stitches.

YF/ YFWD (Yarn Forward) – This is a yarnover between two knit stitches. You'll therefore only need to carry out steps 1 and 2 of the YO instructions on page 69, since the yarn will be in the correct position (at the back) for a knit stitch following the second step.

YRN (Yarn Round Needle) – This is a yarnover between two purl stitches. You'll therefore only need to carry out steps 2 and 3 of the YO instructions on page 69–70 since the yarn will be in the correct position (in front) to begin the second step.

YON (Yarn Over Needle) – This is a yarnover after a purl stitch and before a knit stitch. You'll therefore only need to carry out step 2 of the YO instructions on page 69 since the yarn will be in the correct position (in front) to begin the second step and will end up in the correct position (at the back) after the second step, ready for the knit stitch.
YFRN (Yarn Forward Round Needle) – This is a yarnover after a knit stitch and before a purl stitch. Therefore you need to carry out all three steps of the YO instructions on page 69–70 since the yarn will be in the incorrect position (at the back) to begin the second step and will end up in the incorrect position (at the back) to carry out the purl stitch.

Decreasing

As with increasing, decreasing is also common in knitting patterns. It's used for shaping the crowns of hats, the tops of glove fingers and the necks of garments (amongst lots of other things), so if you're ready to tackle such projects you'd better get familiar with these three common decreasing methods:

THE WORK TOGETHER

If you work two stitches together you are effectively creating one stitch on the right needle while dropping two off the left, hence reducing the number of stitches in the row by one. You can either knit two stitches together (K2tog) or purl two stitches together (P2tog) for the same right-slanting decrease result.

K2tog (Dec 1) Insert the point of the right needle into the next two stitches on the left needle from left to right, front to back. Knit these two stitches together as if they were one stitch.

P2tog (Dec 1) Insert the point of the right needle into the next two stitches on the left needle from right to left, back to front. Purl these two stitches together as if they were one stitch.

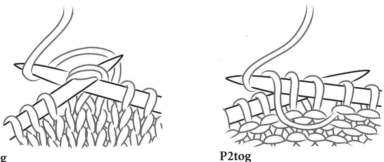

K2tog   P2tog

THE PAIR OF SLIPPERS

By slipping the two stitches you're about to knit together you are effectively twisting them before knitting into the back of them. This helps them to lie flat and creates a left-slanting decrease.

SSK (Slip 1, Slip 1, Knit 1)

Slip the first two stitches off the left needle knitwise, one by one. Insert the point of the left needle from left to right through the front of the two slipped stitches and knit them together as if they were one stitch.

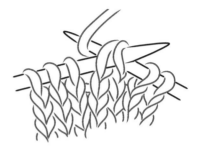

SSP (Slip 1, Slip 1, Purl 1)

Slip the first two stitches off the left needle knitwise, one by one. Insert the point of the left needle from right to left through the back of the two slipped stitches and purl them together as if they were one stitch.

THE PASSOVER

This method produces the same left-slanting decrease as the pair of slippers above, so have a go at both and see which one suits you best.

SKP (Slip 1, Knit 1, Pass Slipped Stitch Over)

Slip the first stitch off the left needle knitwise and knit the following stitch as normal. Insert the point of the left needle into the front of the slipped stitch and lift it over the knitted stitch and off the right needle.

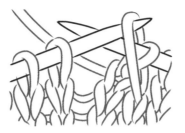

Colour Work

Whilst knitting all in one colour can certainly produce excellent results, you might want to mix things up from time to time and try a few different colours together in one project. There are a few ways of creating multi-coloured knitted fabric that you should have under your belt as a seasoned knitter.

Stripes

Creating different-coloured stripes in your knitting is extremely satis-fying and easy to do; you simply need to introduce a contrasting col-oured yarn at the beginning of a row. To introduce a new yarn colour, cut the yarn you are currently working with, leaving a generous length of tail, and begin knitting the next row with the new yarn, also leaving a tail. These tails will need to be woven into the fabric at the end to neaten them off, but not to worry, we'll teach you how to do that later on (see page 86).

Once you know how to create stripes in your knitting you can go crazy and get a whole lot of colours going on. Before you do, though, there are a few last pieces of information we'd like to share with you, because while they may seem easy, stripes can leave you scratching your head from time to time...

- Don't cut each coloured yarn into a tail if you don't have to – nobody wants to weave in hundreds of tails at the end if they can avoid it! Instead, if the colour you're working is needed for a stripe a little way up your knitting, leave the yarn attached on the side and every time you get to that side, twist it round the yarn you're working with so that it trails neatly up the side of your work until you need it again.
- Change colour in textured knitting with a plain knit row, because if you do this using a purl stitch you will create a little loop of the previous colour yarn around the new stitch. If you are working in a textured stitch – such as moss, rib or cable – make sure you change colour with a pure knit row. While this will interrupt the texture slightly, it will create a clean change of colour and look a lot better than having a dashed line of the contrasting colour along the fabric.

Fair Isle (AKA Stranded Knitting)

Fair Isle is the method of working two or more yarn colours in a single row to create pictures and patterns on a finished piece of knitting. To be all 'matter of fact' about it, Fair Isle knitting is a specific type of stranded knitting which is knit in the round and forms a symmetrical pattern that originated on Fair Isle (a tiny island in northern Scotland, one of the Shetland Islands). If the pattern is not exclusively 'Fair Isle' then it really should be called 'stranded knitting', but the terms have pretty much become interchangeable since people have gotten it wrong over the years, so don't beat yourself up about it!

In stranded knitting you simply knit a number of stitches in one colour then a number of stitches in another, all the while keeping the yarn balls attached to the work and trailing the 'inactive' yarn across

the back of the work until it is required again. The back of stranding knitting looks pretty messy, with lots of strands running along (called 'floats'), so it's advisable to only use this method for items where the inside will not be seen, such as socks or jumpers. If you want to knit a Fair Isle scarf it's a good idea to knit it double width, fold it lengthwise and seam it so the messiness of the floats is hidden on the inside (or add a fleece lining).

It takes a bit of practise to get into the groove of stranded knitting, as there's a lot going on on those needles, but be patient and try out a few different ways of holding the extra yarn(s) until it starts to feel comfortable.

One Yarn at a Time

This might be the easiest method when beginning, but it can be slow and difficult to keep your yarns from twisting mid row, so it's worth giving the other methods a good go before you decide on one technique. Simply pick up and knit the active yarn and drop it when not needed. You want to make sure that you pick up and knit the dominant colour from above the second colour and pick up and knit the second colour from below the dominant colour to keep the floats lying flat.

Both Yarns in One Hand

This method allows you to knit continuously without letting go of the needles. Hold both yarns in one hand (whichever hand is most comfortable to you) and either hold each yarn over different fingers or use a clever device called a 'yarn guide' to hold both yarns, slightly apart, on your index finger. Then knit each colour as required.

One Yarn in Each Hand

This technique is popular if you're only using two colours in one row because holding one yarn in each hand enables a smooth knitting action without the need to let go of the needles. It also leaves the floats lying neatly at the back of the work as the yarn in the right hand always lies above the left and does not get tangled.

Hold the dominant yarn (usually the background yarn) in your right hand, English style (see page 47) and the other colour in your left hand, Continental style (see page 47) then work each independently according to the pattern chart.

Traditional Fair Isle patterns didn't usually call for the knitter to knit more than two or three consecutive stitches before changing colour; this avoids creating long floats at the back which cause uneven tension and have a tendency of getting caught on things. However, over the years stranded knitting has evolved and some patterns require a single colour to be knit for an inch or more, leaving long floats that just aren't good to have around. There's always a solution though, and so a method of weaving in these floats was developed and the evolution of stranding knitting continues.

> **GRANNY'S PURL OF WISDOM**
>
> Make sure you spread out the stitches on your right needle every time you change colour to ensure the strand your are introducing has the same tension as the stitches it is stretching behind. This will stop your fabric puckering and help it lie flat.

The method of weaving in floats is slightly different depending on which yarn is active and whether you are working on a knit or purl side.

Begin by picking up and holding the yarn that you are about to weave in (the one that will become the float) in your spare hand. Note than this will already be the case if you're working with one yarn in each hand.

Next follow whichever of the following 4 methods is most suitable to the side you are working on and the position of your active and floating yarns (beware: they're not for the faint hearted)...

Weaving in on the KNIT side

- **Weaving in when the floating yarn is in your LEFT hand and the active yarn is in your RIGHT hand**
1. Insert your right needle into the next stitch knitwise.
2. Wrap the yarn in your left hand (the float) clockwise around the right needle and hold on the left hand side.
3. Wrap the yarn in your right hand (the active yarn) anti-clockwise around the right needle and hold on the right hand side.
4. Complete your knit stitch by pulling the loop of active yarn on the right needle back through the stitch (being careful not to bring the float through with it).

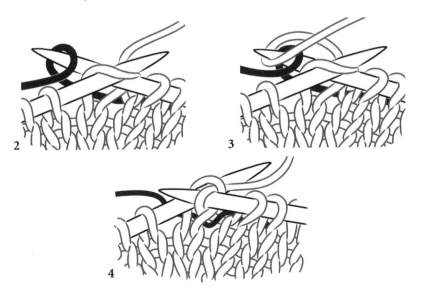

- **Weaving in when the floating yarn is in your RIGHT hand and the active yarn is in your LEFT hand**
1. Insert your right needle into the next stitch knitwise.
2. Wrap the yarn in your right hand (the float) anti-clockwise around the right needle and hold on the right hand side.
3. Wrap the yarn in your left hand (the active yarn) anti-clockwise around the right needle and hold on the left hand side.
4. Unwrap the yarn in your right hand (the float) back off the right needle.
5. Complete your knit stitch by pulling the loop of active yarn on the right needle back through the stitch.

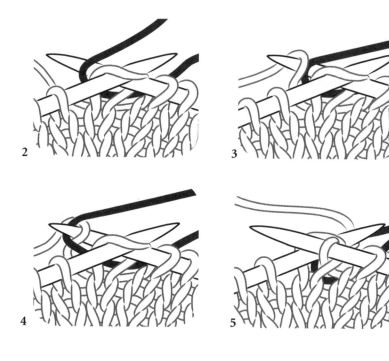

Weaving in on the PURL side

- **Weaving in when the floating yarn is in your LEFT hand and the active yarn is in your RIGHT hand**

1. Insert your right needle into the next stitch purlwise.
2. Wrap the yarn in your left hand (the float) anti-clockwise around the right needle and hold on the left hand side.
3. Wrap the yarn in your right hand (the active yarn) anti-clockwise around the right needle and hold on the right hand side.
4. Complete your purl stitch by pulling the loop of active yarn on the right needle back through the stitch (being careful not the bring the float through with it).

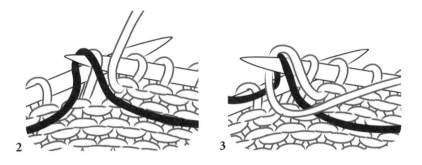

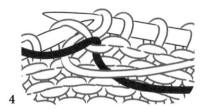

- **Weaving in when the floating yarn is in your RIGHT hand and the active yarn is in your LEFT hand**
1. Insert your right needle into the next stitch purlwise.
2. Wrap the yarn in your right hand (the float) clockwise around the right needle and hold on the right hand side.
3. Wrap the yarn in your left hand (the active yarn) anti-clockwise around the right needle and hold on the left hand side.
4. Unwrap the yarn in your right hand (the float) back off the right needle.
5. Complete your purl stitch by pulling the loop of active yarn on the right needle back through the stitch.

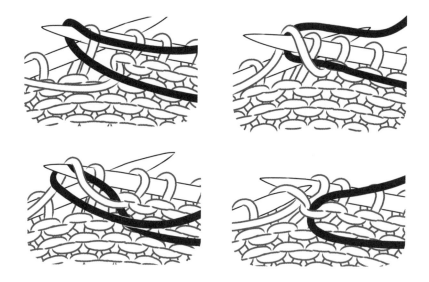

Intarsia

Another way to spice up your knits with splashes of colour is by using the technique of intarsia. It is great for creating blocks of colour and is how pictures (think Colin Firth's reindeer jumper in *Bridget Jones' Diary*) are created in a piece of knitting. Like Fair Isle, intarsia involves two or more yarn colours in the same row, but unlike Fair Isle it doesn't

involve trailing the strands across the back of the work. Instead, blocks of colour are worked using their own balls of yarn and are joined by twisting yarns at the point of a colour change along a row.

Each area of colour needs its own ball of yarn, so it is a good idea to start off by winding a suitable length of the yarn required for each large block around a bobbin, which prevents a tangled mess developing behind your work. For small sections of colour you can just cut an adequate length (about three times the width of the stitches needing to be worked), and leave it hanging behind your work when it's not being used. Once prepared, you'll need to know these few simple techniques and you'll be knitting your very own Van Gogh in no time!

JOINING A NEW COLOUR

1. Insert the point of your right needle into the next stitch.
2. Hold a 10cm or so tail of the new colour to the left, and with your right hand lay it over the point of your right needle and wrap it anti-clockwise around the old yarn strand.
3. Complete your knit or purl stitch as normal, pulling the tail of the new yarn upwards to avoid bringing it back through the loop with the new stitch.
4. Let the tail drop behind the work and continue working with the new colour.

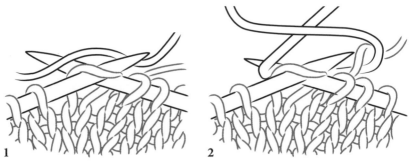

Once a colour has been joined in it can be used on following rows by picking it up from under and twisting it round the old yarn as follows:

CHANGING COLOURS ON A KNIT ROW

1. Insert the point of your right needle into the next stitch knitwise.
2. Hold the old yarn to the left and bring the new yarn up and behind the old yarn to twist the yarns together.
3. Knit the stitch using the new yarn.

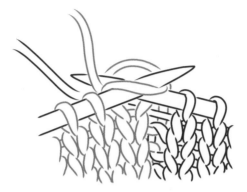

CHANGING COLOURS ON A PURL ROW

1. Insert the point of your right needle into the next stitch purlwise.
2. Hold the old yarn to the left and bring the new yarn up and in front of the old yarn to twist the yarns together.
3. Purl the stitch using the new yarn.

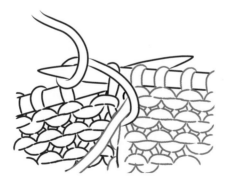

I've Started so I'll Finish

A mistake that many a newbie knitter makes is thinking that once you've completed all the knitting in your pattern, you're done. Well, as much as we hate to say it, there is still more to do. We'd like to tell you that the good stuff is still to come, but we'd be lying.

'Finishing', as we call it in the knitting world, is often considered the most tedious part of a project, because by the time you've got to that point you're absolutely gagging to complete the work so that you can flaunt your new handmade knit in front of all your friends. Please don't let that put you off, though, some people we've come across love it. Each to their own.

What we will say about it is – boy, it is satisfying! It's a great feeling after you've spent loads of hours knitting your fabric to finish it with the perfectly invisible seams it deserves, as if you knitted the whole garment on some kind of magic needles all in one go! Take your time finishing your projects and you will be rewarded in the long term.

Weaving in Yarn Ends

It doesn't matter how simple the project you've undertaken, you're going to be lumped with at least two yarn ends that will need to be woven into your work at the end. While a one-colour, knitted coaster will only have a couple of stray yarn ends to neaten away, a multi-coloured stripy jumper will have loads. The good news is that these ends are easy to weave in and if you do them as you go along it will take a bit of the pain away when you finish.

Using a large-eyed yarn needle, thread the loose end and weave it in and out of the bumps at the back of your work, or up the seam if there is space (you don't want multiple ends crossing along the seam). There is no correct way to weave in these ends but the yarn is more easily disguised in a purl stitch, so use these if you can find them. Try to move up and down a row or two – the end is less likely to pull out if the fabric is stretched. Once about 10cm of the end has been woven in, cut it close to the fabric and give yourself a pat on the back before moving on to the other hundred left to do!

Blocking

Blocking is a finishing method used to 'set' a piece of knitted fabric. It can reshape a fabric to match the pattern's exact measurements, straighten out an intarsia or Fair Isle fabric, flatten a heavily textured fabric or open out a lacy one. Blocking is your friend, your ally, the icing on your cake; covering up all those little discrepancies in your knitting that may or may not be your fault. So listen carefully...

To block a piece of knitted fabric you'll first need to find yourself a flat, soft surface. An ironing board will do the trick for smaller fabric pieces, but if your fabric is larger than will fit on your ironing board (or you need it for that basket full of ironing you've been meaning to do) you'll need to get creative and look around your house for another solution. A spare bed, flat sofa cushion, even your carpet will do – it just needs to be somewhere where the fabric can remain undisturbed for a few hours. Next, take a towel bigger than the fabric you are blocking and lay it over your flat surface.

To begin blocking we usually use our hands to stretch the fabric in all directions a few times over, which should help the stitches wriggle into place and even themselves out. Be careful not to overstretch the fabric, though, just pull it as gently as you can while still getting results.

Next, lay your fabric down on the towel, wrong side up, and place a rust-proof pin every two or three centimetres around the edge to hold the fabric in place. Now it's at this point that you can stretch and shape the fabric into exactly the measurement given in the pattern, to ensure the finished garment fits perfectly. Be reasonable when reshaping, though, if your fabric pieces are way off what the pattern suggests you should probably recheck your tension and make sure you've followed the correct size instructions. Once pinned, spray your fabric with water (we tend to use empty cleaning product spray bottles for this) and leave it until it is completely dry before unpinning and admiring it.

Seaming

In many knitting projects the final instructions will be to join the various knitted pieces together. This is called seaming. There are loads of different ways to seam, which one you use is dependent on the direction in which the pieces need to be joined. The ultimate goal is to create a seam that is completely invisible – which is not too hard to achieve once you've got a few techniques under your belt. It also helps to use the same yarn with which you knitted the pieces when sewing them together – unless it breaks easily, in which case use a more robust yarn of a similar colour.

VERTICAL SEAMING
Invisibly joining two sides of knitting fabric is easy peasy lemon squeezy once you learn a simple technique called the mattress stitch. It's always a good idea to pin your pieces together before seaming them, as the holy grail of invisible seaming is more easily achieved when the stitches on each piece are perfectly aligned. Begin by placing your two

pieces side by side, with the edges you are going to join touching. Pin the top and bottom of the length, and place a pin every few centimetres along the join, making sure you have the same number of stitches between pins.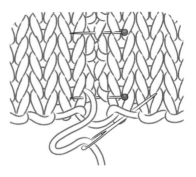

Either using the long tail from your cast on or a fresh piece of yarn threaded onto a large-eyed needle, join the bottom corners of the pieces by feeding the needle from back to front into one corner and again through the other using a figure of eight action.

JOINING STOCKING STITCH USING MATTRESS STITCH

If you look carefully at the edge of your stocking stitch piece you will see a column of uneven edge stitches. Not very pretty, are they? The next column in, and all other col- 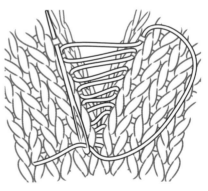 umns, however, should be beautiful vertical chains of little 'v's made up of your carefully worked knit stitches. The idea when joining stocking stitch is to pull the edges together just before the first beauti- ful column of each piece and hide the nasty edge stitches on the inside of your work.

If you look between the edge column of stitches and the first straight column of stitches, you will see that they are joined with a horizontal bar of yarn. All you need to do to join two pieces of stocking stitch is to work your yarn needle under- neath this bar on one piece, carry it across to the other piece and work it underneath the corresponding bar on the that piece. Start from the bottom and work all the way up the edges, joining each row individu- ally to bring the two sides together in perfect matrimony.

JOINING GARTER STITCH USING MATTRESS STITCH

If you've got two pieces of garter stitch to join vertically, it is very easy to create an invisible seam by binding stitches together from either edge. If you take a close look at the edge of a piece of garter stitch you'll see that the first stitch (purl) consists of a top loop and a bottom loop.

To seam two garter edges, simply work your needle underneath the top loop on one piece, carry it across to the other piece and work it underneath the bottom loop of the corresponding stitch on that piece. Do this for each purl row all the way up your seam and Bob's your uncle.

NB you use the same method for joining garter stitch as you would do for joining reverse stocking stitch.

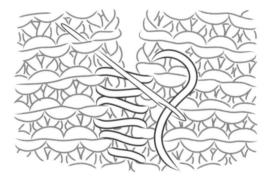

JOINING RIB STITCH

Joining rib stitch is a little bit trickier. The idea is to seam the ribbing in a way that doesn't disturb the pattern, so that the ribbing looks continuous all the way around. In 1 x 1 rib this is fairly simple to do.

Joining knit to knit in 1 x 1 rib

Work your needle through the bottom loop of the first purl stitch on one piece, then through the top loop of the first purl stitch on the corresponding row of the other piece. This will create a whole purl stitch from two halves, one from each piece.

Joining purl to purl in 1 x 1 rib

Work your needle through the horizontal bar in the centre of the first knit stitch on one piece, then through the centre of the first knit stitch on the corresponding row of the other piece. This will create a whole knit stitch from two halves, one from each piece.

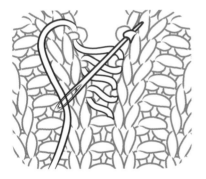

Joining knit to knit in 1 x 1 rib

Joining purl to purl in 1 x 1 rib

Joining knit to purl in 1x1 rib (and vice versa)

Either... skip the first stitch on the piece with the knit stitch at its edge and join the two pieces, continuing as if you are joining purl to purl.

Or... skip the first stitch on the piece with the purl stitch at its edge and continue as if you are joining knit to knit.

HORIZONTAL SEAMING

Horizontal seaming is needed when you're trying to join two cast on/off edges, such as joining two ends of a scarf to make a snood. For a completely successful join you want to make sure you have the same number of stitches on each piece, otherwise you need to do as we suggested for vertical seaming and skip a few stitches as you go along.

First pin your pieces together, right side up, and use the long tail from the cast on/off to join the two corners together as described earlier.

Feed the yarn under the first stitch of the first row on one piece, carry it across and feed it under the corresponding stitch on the other piece. If you look closely you will have created a 'v' shape with the thread. Does this look similar to any stitch you know? That's right, if you pull the thread only as tight as is needed to make the new 'v' shape the same size as the knit stitches at the edge of the piece, you have made your very own faux-knit stitch – congratulations! When you seam all along it will look like a neat row of knit stitches. Genius!

KITCHENER STITCH (AKA GRAFTING)

Now here's a bit of trivia about the old Kitchener stitch which will impress your friends at your next knitting circle... This stitch was named after Lord Kitchener (AKA Field Marshal Horatio Herbert Kitchener or 1st Earl Kitchener), a British Field Marshal who, apart from his central role in WWI, will always be remembered amongst us knitting folk as the helpful chap who introduced a sock pattern featuring the seamless join now known as the Kitchener stitch!

Yep, that's right, whilst encouraging the women to knit for the war effort this proconsul also solved the problem of uncomfortable toe seams. What a guy!

For a truly invisible horizontal seam there's nothing out there quite like 'The Kitchener'. It takes a bit of concentration but it's not hard once you get the hang of it. Unfortunately for some seams, you can only do this stitch between two sets of 'live' stitches (stitches that haven't been cast off), and the one golden rule is to make absolutely sure that you have the same number of stitches on each piece you are joining. If you're planning on doing a Kitchener seam, just ignore the pattern when it says to cast off and either leave the stitches on the needle or transfer them to a stitch holder until the second piece is ready – which is when you'll need to transfer them back onto the needle.

1. Prepare for seaming by holding the two needles together (either pointing to the left or right depending on your preference) so that the knitted pieces are wrong side facing. Thread the long yarn tail (at least three times the width of the seam required) onto a yarn needle.
2. Insert your yarn needle into the first stitch on the front needle purlwise, pull the yarn through so that it is not too tight and leave the stitch on the needle.
3. Insert your yarn needle into the first stitch on the back needle knitwise, pull the yarn through and leave the stitch on the needle.
4. Insert your yarn needle into the first stitch on the front needle knitwise, pull the yarn through and slip the stitch off the needle.
5. Insert the yarn needle into the next stitch on the front needle purlwise, pull the yarn through but leave the stitch on the needle.

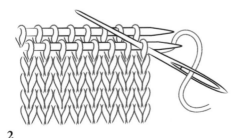

2

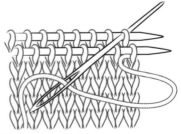

3 (steps overleaf)

6. Insert the yarn needle into the first stitch on the back needle purlwise, pull the yarn through and slip the stitch off the needle.
7. Insert the yarn needle into the next stitch on the back needle knitwise, pull the yarn through but leave the stitch on the needle.
8. Repeat steps 4–7 for each corresponding stitch along the whole edge.

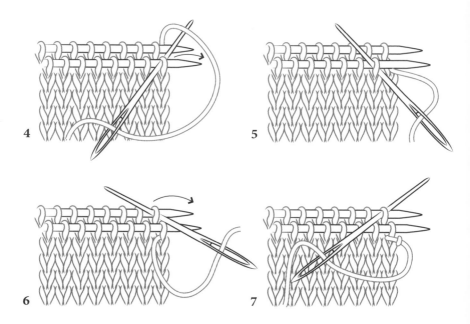

Look carefully at what you have just achieved – you should be over the moon to see that you've created an extra row of 'v' shapes which are perfectly aligned with the knit rows on both pieces of fabric. Seamless. Invisible. Exquisite.

GRANNY'S
PURL OF WISDOM

If your Kitchener stitch seam is not quite as invisible as you had hoped and the 'v's are differing sizes along the row, don't fret – with a bit of care you can fix it...

Place the joined fabric on a flat surface and, starting where you began your seam and moving along it, use the tip of your yarn needle to adjust the v shapes to match the rows above and below. Loose yarn from any excess tension can be carried along the seam and pulled taut using the tail at the end of the seam.

BACK STITCH

Ah, the good old back stitch; we have a love–hate relationship! It's probably the easiest and quickest way to seam two pieces of knitting together, but don't be fooled, it has its drawbacks. Back stitch creates a very firm, bulky seam that has its uses (such as strengthening the bottom seam of a bag), but often leaves a very obvious, uneven seam. It can, however, be used to seam two pieces of knitting at any orientation to each other. As with most things knitting, just use your head – if the seam is in a very prominent position on the garment a bulky back stitch seam is probably not a great idea.

1. Begin by aligning the edges you want to seam, by placing the knitted pieces one on top of the other with the right sides together. Pin together.
2. Join the two corners by inserting the needle through both layers from back to front a few stitches in from the side edges and however far down you are planning on making the seam. Take the yarn around the side edges and back through the point from which it last emerged a couple of times, leaving it at the back.

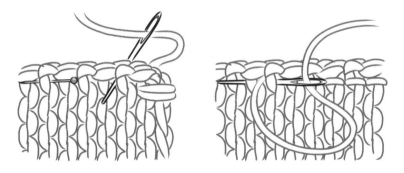

3. Insert the needle two stitches along from where the yarn last emerged, from back to front. Insert the needle two stitches back along the seam, where the previous stitch began.
4. Repeat step 3 all the way along the seam and finish off by joining the corners as you did in step 2.

VERTICAL TO HORIZONTAL

Vertical to horizontal seaming is used when joining a cast-off edge with a side edge – most commonly when attaching a sleeve into an armhole. This technique is a combination of the vertical and horizontal seam stitches we taught you earlier, so if you were listening carefully you should have this one down. If not, slap yourself on the wrist and listen up!

1. Place your two pieces of fabric on a flat surface, with the right sides up, and pin together the edges you want to join. Thread your yarn needle with the long tail from the cast off.
2. Work the yarn needle under the first stitch of the first row on the cast-off piece.
3. Work your yarn needle underneath the bar between the first and second stitches on the side piece. (Note that because there are usually more rows per centimetre than stitches you will occasionally need to work your needle under two bars on the side edge to prevent the cast-off edge puckering.)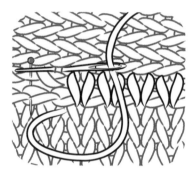
4. Repeat steps 2 and 3 carefully, joining one or two side rows with each cast-off stitch.

PICKING UP STITCHES

There will come a time when your pattern calls for you to 'pick up' some stitches. We at Grannies, Inc. got together to discuss this point and we cannot quite work out whether 'picking up a stitch' is the opposite of 'dropping a stitch'. It is in the respect that when you drop a stitch you lose one off your needle, and when you pick up a stitch you gain one, but one is by accident and considered an error in knitting and the other is not. Hmmm, you can debate that one at your next knitting circle.

Back to the technique in question, though, picking up stitches is most commonly used when adding a neck to a jumper or any type of border to your knitting.

Start by holding your work, right side facing, in your left hand and your needle in your right. Depending on which edge you need to pick up stitches from, follow the directions below.

From a cast off edge
Insert your needle into the centre of the first stitch of the last row before the cast off. Wrap your yarn anti-clockwise around the needle tip and bring the loop back through the stitch just as if you were doing a regular knit stitch. Repeat for as many stitches as you need to pick up, each time inserting your needle into the centre of the next stitch.

From a side edge
Insert your needle between the first and second stitches of the side edge. Wrap your yarn anti-clockwise around the needle tip and bring the loop back through the stitch just as if you were doing a regular knit stitch. Repeat along the side edge for as many stitches as you need to pick up, inserting your needle one or two rows along each time. You will often find that you need to pick up fewer stitches than there are rows. To make sure your picked-up stitches align perfectly with the piece they are adjoining, miss out a row every so often to stretch the stitches over the length of the edge.

Accidents Happen

Let's all be honest with ourselves here, we are far from perfect. We have all accidentally washed a load of whites with one red sock. We have all nudged the car behind (and in front) when reverse parking. And by golly we have certainly dropped a stitch or two. If you haven't got Jimmy Savile locked up in your wardrobe, you are going to have to learn a few techniques to get you out of whichever sticky situation you have got yourself into.

Picking up Dropped Stitches

We do it all the time, don't worry about it. When you're trying to watch the telly or read a book whilst knitting away it is almost inevitable that you'll miss a stitch, knit the next one and drop the missed one off the end of your needle. The trick here is not to ignore the problem; it's not going to go away, the stitch is not going to magically weave itself back into its neighbouring stitches, and one thing is for sure – it will only get worse with time. When you spot the mistake, deal with it.

Start by working up to the point where the dropped stitch is in between your needles and follow the instructions below, depending on how quick you were to spot it.

Picking up a knit stitch that has dropped one row...

1. Insert your right needle from front to back through the dropped stitch and underneath the loose strand of yarn behind it.
2. Using the left needle, lift the dropped stitch over the strand and drop it off the right needle at the back.

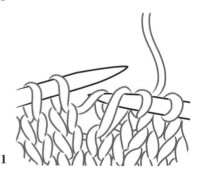

1

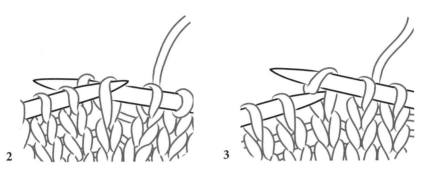

2

3

3. Lastly, insert the tip of your left needle into the restored stitch on the right needle, from right to left, and slip it from the right to the left needle.

Picking up a purl stitch that has dropped one row...
1. Insert your right needle from back to front through the dropped stitch and underneath the loose strand of yarn in front of it.
2. Using the left needle, lift the dropped stitch over the strand and drop it off the right needle at the front.
3. Lastly, insert the tip of your left needle into the restored stitch on the right needle, from left to right, and slip it from the right to the left needle.

1

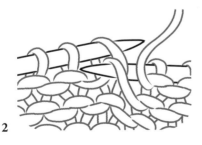

2

3

Picking up a number of dropped knit stitches more than one row below...

You'll notice that you've dropped a number of stitches by the tell-tale ladder that has appeared down your work. At the base this ladder you will find a stray loop – the guilty one. What you want to do is pull the first ladder rung through this loop from back to front. For this task it's really useful to use a crochet hook, but if you don't have one lying around you can always use the tip of a knitting or yarn needle.

Insert your hook or needle through the loop from front to back and under the first rung of the ladder. Bring it back out of the loop, taking the rung with it and leaving the new loop on the needle. Now, pull the next rung of the ladder through the loop that is already on the needle and repeat this all the way up your ladder until all your knit stitches are restored. Transfer the last loop on the crochet hook or spare needle onto your working needle and away you go.

If you notice the dreaded ladder that should in fact have been a lovely column of purl stitches, simply turn your work around and repair the dropped stitches as explained on the previous page before turning your work back around and continuing as you were.

Picking up a number of dropped knit AND purl stitches more than one row below...

If you're knitting a textured pattern such as moss stitch and one of your stitches goes astray, unnoticed, you will need to pick up the dropped stitches according to which stitch they were supposed to be: knit or purl. If you're picking up a knit stitch, do as described before and insert your hook or needle through the front of the loop, catch the first ladder rung and pull it forwards through the loop. When you get to a purl stitch that needs picking up, remove your hook or needle, pinch the loop so that it doesn't escape down the ladder again, turn your work around and repair it as you did the knit stitch.

Unravelling a single row

If you've realised you've made a mistake earlier in the row that you are knitting, such as knitting when you should have been purling or decreasing at the wrong point, don't worry, you haven't ruined your work. All you need to do is to undo each stitch back to the point where you made the mistake.

To undo a knit or a purl stitch, insert your left needle from front to back into the stitch below the first loop on the right needle, slip the loop off the right needle and pull the working yarn so that the loop disappears altogether.

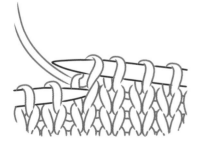

Undoing knit stitch

Undoing purl stitch

Unravelling several rows

When you notice a mistake a few rows or more down your work (we call it the 'devil row') you're going to have to unravel the work all the way down to that point to fix it. You can choose to ignore it and hope no one notices, but trust us, you will always know it's there. It's a frustrating task but you've got to weigh up whether it's worth doing it or not in the long run.

You could pull out your needle full of stitches, pull at the tail until you arrive at the devil row and reinsert you needle, however this is a risky method that often results in dropped stitches. So try the following method instead.

Take a needle a couple of sizes smaller than the ones you are working with and weave the point from back to front through each stitch of the row below the devil row. Slip all the stitches off the working needle and pull the yarn to unravel all stitches down to the spare needle. If the working yarn ends up at the wrong end of the spare needle, simply transfer the stitches back onto your working needle before continuing to knit. Otherwise, you can continue knitting straight from the spare needle.

Decorating your knitting

Once you've mastered the art of knitting and you've run out of things to do with yarn you'll be happy to hear there are a few decorative features that can be made with your odds and ends of leftover yarn and appended to your finished pieces to give them that something extra. You can put those needles down for a while and get creative in a few other ways.

Pom-poms

We probably learned to make pom-poms before we learned to knit. They're really easy and fun to make, so grab yourself a cereal box, some scissors and some yarn and let's get going.

To make a pom-pom, cut two circles of cardboard with a diameter approximately the same size as the diameter of the pom-pom you're looking to make. Cut a round hole in the centre about half the size of total diameter and wind lengths of yarn round and round the cardboard 'doughnut' until you can't fit any more yarn through the hole in the centre (see illustration 1 overleaf) you will need to use a darning needle to get the last bits through the middle).

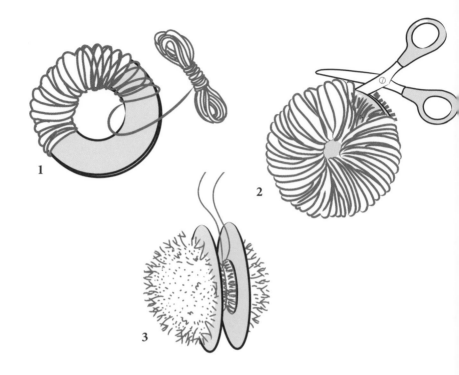

1

2

3

Choose a point somewhere around the circumference of the circle and push apart the yarn to expose the cardboard below. Place the point of the scissors horizontally (step 2 above) between the two pieces of cardboard and cut through the bound edge of the yarn, keeping the scissors between the two circles of cardboard all the time. When you have gone all the way round, wrap a length of yarn tightly round between the two card circles and knot firmly, leaving two good lengths of yarn to use to attach the pom-pom to your piece. Cut away the cardboard and trim the pom-pom (step 3 above) to smooth out any uneven edges (except for the two attachment strands).

GRANNY'S
PURL OF WISDOM

Life's way too short to be cutting out circles of cardboard. If you make pom-poms often it's probably worth investing in a pom-pom maker to save yourself a bit of work. A pom-pom maker consists of reusable plastic rings of varying sizes that can be used instead of cardboard.

Attach your pom-pom to your knitting using a large-eyed needle, knot the two strands on the wrong side of your work and weave in the ends.

Fringes

Perfect for adding a bit of length to your scarves, fringes are really easy to make and give nervous people something to twirl around their fingers!

Simply cut a number of pieces of yarn that are double the length of the finished fringe you want. Fold these in half to create a loop and, using a crochet hook, pull the loop a little way through the edge of your knitting from front to back. Slip the ends of the strands through the loop at the back and pull tightly to create a neat knot at the scarf's edge. Repeat at regular intervals all the way along the edge of your knitting and finish by trimming the strands to ensure they are all the same length. Hey presto – you've got yourself a fringe!

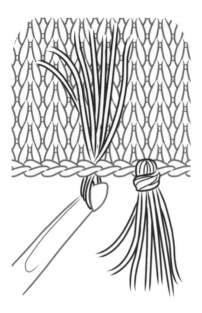

Tassels

Tassels are great way to add decoration to your knitwear, whether they are for your burlesque accessories or replica 'Tommy Cooper' hat.

You begin in the same way as you did for the fringe, by cutting a number of pieces of yarn that are double the length of the tassel you want, then folding them in half. Take another length of yarn, fold it in half and wrap it around the centre fold of the tassel strands. Bring the two ends of the doubled-over strand through the loop at its centre and pull to tighten. Take another length of yarn and wrap it round and round the strands of the tassel near the top, knot, and, using a large-eyed needle, pull the ends back through the knot and downwards so that they disappear into the tassel. Finally, trim the tassel to make it all neat and tidy and attach it to your knitwear.

I-Cord

Unlike the iPod or iPad, the i-cord was not created by those boffins at Apple but by a lovely British-born lady called Elizabeth Zimmerman, who also happened to revolutionise the modern practice of knitting. What a lady she was! An i-cord (or 'idiot cord', as it's sometimes known) is a cord knitted on two double-pointed needles and is useful for a multitude of purposes, including bag handles, belts and headbands. Although it's knit on double pointers, you don't really need to know anything about circular knitting to be able to do this, so don't sweat it. Just remember to use around about the recommended needle size for the yarn, unless specifically told not to in the pattern.

1. Using double-pointed needles, cast on as many stitches as your pattern calls for (usually 3–5).
2. Knit one row but do not turn.
3. Slide the stitches to the other end of the needle and, without turning, hold this needle in your left hand.
4. Knit the stitches on the left needle, pulling the tail tightly on the first stitch as it will be coming from the left-most stitch. Do not turn.
5. Repeat steps 3 and 4 until you have the desired length cord.
6. Cast off.

And there you have it, a quickly and easily made cord to do with what you wish.

Caring for Your Knits

Although knitting is a labour of love for most, nobody likes to see their hard work go to waste. Your finished garments should be cared for with as much love as you knit them, otherwise their shelf life will deteriorate rapidly. Properly handled knitwear can last forever, which will either impress or embarrass your kids or friend in years to come. Below are some tips, and you can also refer to care instructions on pages 25–26.

Washing

Wash your knitwear according to the ball bands of the yarn used to make it. If you have used more than one yarn, follow the instructions of the yarn with the softest approach, rather than the easiest. If you're not sure or the instructions are unknown, always hand wash knitted garments.

To hand wash knitwear...

1. Lay your knitwear in a bath or sink of lukewarm water mixed with the recommended amount of handwash detergent.
2. Gently squeeze the fabric to work the soap through the fibres.
3. Leave it soak for a few minutes.
4. Rinse your knitwear in fresh running water, gently squeezing the fabric but not lifting it, until the water runs clear of suds.

5. Gently squeeze out any excess water (don't be tempted to wring the water out as it could damage the shaping completely).
6. Lift the knitwear out of the sink or bath, supporting its weight, then lay it flat on a towel and roll tightly to squeeze out any further water.

To machine wash your knitwear...
1. Put your knitting in a delicates wash bag (you can use a pillowcase, knotted at the end, if you haven't a wash bag handy).
2. Put the wash bag inside the drum and wash on the delicate cycle.
3. Pace up and down while debating whether you should have hand washed the piece of knitwear.
4. Remove as soon as the cycle is complete and lay it flat to dry (feeling a bit smug that you didn't waste your time hand washing).

> **GRANNY'S PURL OF WISDOM**
>
> If you're knitting for someone else (and what a lucky person they are), it's a good idea to include a care card so the recipient knows exactly how the knitwear should be cared for. Failing that, throw in one of the bands from the yarn balls, which should have the care instructions already printed out for you.

Drying

Never, EVER, put your knitwear in the dryer. Just don't. Don't dry it on coat hangers either, unless you're expecting a growth spurt any time soon.

1. Lay your knitwear on a towel big enough to accommodate it.
2. Gently pull and push the fabric into its original shape.
3. Be patient and wait until it is completely dry (depending on your environment, this could take days).
4. Strut about in it as if it was brand new.

Storing your Knitwear

Knitwear to a moth is like pasta to an Italian. They absolutely love it! Given free reign moths will go at your knitwear day in day out and you'll find it disintegrates in your hands when you next go to put it on. Soiled knitwear is even tastier to them, so make sure you wash and dry knitwear thoroughly before storing. You can buy special moth bags for storing knitwear, but failing that use a fabric bag and include some kind of moth repellent to make extra, extra sure those darn insects don't feast on your hard work.

If I'm Sittin' I'm Knittin'

20 PATTERNS TO KEEP YOUR FINGERS BUSY*

*NOTE: For alternative wools to the Grannies, Inc. yarns, please see page 184.

Cable Beanie

MATERIALS

Grannies, Inc. Ever So Warm Chunky Yarn (100% merino wool)*

Colourway 1
- A: 1 x 50g hank Catkin
- B: 1 x 50g hank Sienna
- C: 1 x 50g hank Olive

Colourway 2
- A: 2 x 50g hank Hot Pink

1 pair of UK size 0 (8mm) circular needles, 40cm length
1 cable needle

TENSION

14 sts and 20 rows to 4in (10cm) measured over large size cable panel using UK size 0 (8mm) needles.

13 sts and 18 rows to 10cm measured over 1x1 rib using UK size 0 (8mm) needles.

MEASUREMENTS

Size	To fit head circumference (cm):	Approx. length from rim to crown (cm):
Small	50–53	17
Medium	54–57	19
Large	58–61	21
X-Large	62–65	23

Colourway

Colourway 1: The colourway for this beanie consists of 10 consecutive stripes of the A, B and C yarn colours. Cast on using yarn A, then change colour every 3 [3: 4: 4] rounds for the first 9 stripes and complete the beanie with one final stripe of 5 [8: 3: 6] rounds (including crown-shaping rounds).

Colourway 2: Use yarn A throughout.

Pattern

Cast on 48 [54: 60: 66] sts.
1st and 2nd round: *K4, P1, K2 [3: 4: 5], P1, rep from * to end.
3rd round: *C4F, P1, K2 [3: 4: 5], P1, rep from * to end.
4th round: *K4, P1, K2 [3: 4: 5], P1, rep from * to end.
(The first 4 rounds make up the cable panel.)
Continue this cable panel for another 21 [23: 26: 28] rounds.

Shape crown
1st round: (Work cable panel for 6 [7: 8: 9] sts, work 2tog) 6 times.
    42 [48: 54: 60] sts.
2nd round: (Work cable panel for 5 [6: 7: 8] sts, work 2tog) 6 times.
    36 [42: 48: 54] sts.
3rd round: (Work cable panel for 4 [5: 6: 7] sts, work 2tog) 6 times.
    30 [36: 42: 48] sts.
4th round: (Work cable panel for 3 [4: 5: 6] sts, work 2tog) 6 times.
    24 [30: 36: 42] sts.
5th round: (Work cable panel for 2 [3: 4: 5] sts, work 2tog) 6 times.
    18 [24: 30: 36] sts.
6th round: (Work cable panel for 1 [2: 3: 4] sts, work 2tog) 6 times.
    12 [18: 24: 30] sts.
7th round: (Work cable panel for 0 [1: 2: 3] sts, work 2tog) 6 times.
    6 [12: 18: 24] sts.

Medium, large and x-large sizes only

8th round: (Work cable panel for - [0: 1: 2] sts, work 2tog) 6 times. - [6: 12: 18] sts.

Large and x-large sizes only

9th round: (Work cable panel for - [-: 0: 1] sts, work 2tog) 6 times. - [-: 6: 12] sts.

X-large size only

10th round: (Work cable panel for - [-: -: 0] sts, work 2tog) 6 times. - [-: -: 6] sts.

All sizes

Break yarn, thread through remaining stitches and fasten off.

To finish

Weave in all ends.

Baggie Beanie

MATERIALS

Grannies, Inc. Ever So Warm Chunky Yarn (100% merino wool)

Colourway 1
- A: 1 x 50g hank Catkin
- B: 1 x 50g hank Sky

Colourway 2
- A: 2 x 50g hanks Turquoise

1 pair of UK size 0 (8mm) circular needles, 40cm length

1 pair of UK size 000 (10mm) circular needles, 40cm length

TENSION

11 sts and 15 rows to 10cm measured over st st using UK size 000 (10mm) needles.

13 sts and 18 rows to 10cm measured over 1x1 rib using UK size 0 (8mm) needles.

MEASUREMENTS

Size	To fit head circumference (cm):	Approx. length from rim to crown (cm):
Small	50–53	25
Medium	54–57	27
Large	58–61	29
X-Large	62–65	31

Pattern

Yarn A: Using size 8mm circular needles, cast on 48 [54: 60: 66] sts.
1st round: (K1, P1) until end of round (1x1 rib).
Work in 1x1 rib for another 9 rounds.
Change to size 10mm circular needles and K 2 rounds.
Yarn B: K 19 [21: 22: 23] rounds.

Shape crown
1st round: (K6 [7: 8: 9], work 2tog) 6 times. 42 [48: 54: 60] sts.
2nd round: (K5 [6: 7: 8], work 2tog) 6 times. 36 [42: 48: 54] sts.
3rd round: (K4 [5: 6: 7], work 2tog) 6 times. 30 [36: 42: 48] sts.
4th round: (K3 [4: 5: 6], work 2tog) 6 times. 24 [30: 36: 42] sts.
5th round: (K2 [3: 4: 5], work 2tog) 6 times. 18 [24: 30: 36] sts.
6th round: (K1 [2: 3: 4], work 2tog) 6 times. 12 [18: 24: 30] sts.
7th round: (K0 [1: 2: 3], work 2tog) 6 times. 6 [12: 18: 24] sts.

Medium, large and x-large sizes only
8th round: (K- [0: 1: 2], work 2tog) 6 times. - [6: 12: 18] sts.

Large and x-large sizes only
9th round: (K- [-: 0: 1], work 2tog) 6 times. - [-: 6: 12] sts.

X-large size only
10th round: (K- [-: -: 0], work 2tog) 6 times. - [-: -: 6] sts.

All sizes
Break yarn, thread through remaining stitches and fasten off.

To finish

Weave in all ends. Make a pom-pom (see page 103–4) using yarn A or B
or a combination of both and attach to the top of your beanie.

Snowflake Earflapper

MATERIALS

Grannies, Inc. Ever So Warm
Chunky Yarn (100% merino
wool)
- A: 1 x 50g hank Salmon
- B: 1 x 50g hank Lightning
1 pair of UK size 0 (8mm) circular
needles, 40cm length

TENSION

12 sts and 18 rows to 10cm
measured over st st using UK size 0
(8mm) needles.

MEASUREMENTS

To fit head circumference 53–58cm.

Pattern

To make the ear flaps

Using either circular or straight 8mm needles (knitting flat) cable cast
on 6 sts.
Yarn A:

    Row 1: K

    Row 2: P

    Row 3: M1, K to last st, M1   (8 sts)

    Row 4: P

    Row 5: M1, K to last st, M1   (10 sts)

    Row 6: P

    Row 7: M1, K to last st, M1   (12 sts)

    Row 8: P

    Row 9: K

    Row 10: P

    Row 11: M1, K to last st, M1   (14 sts)

    Row 12: P

    Row 13: K

    Row 14: P

Row 15: M1, K to last st, M1
    (16 sts)
Row 16: P
Row 17: K
Row 18: P Cut thread and
    weave in.

Repeat instructions to make
a second ear flap and transfer
both to a spare needle.

To make the hat
Yarn A:
Cable cast (3 sts)
Transfer one ear flap onto the
8mm circular needle (ear flap
should be purl side facing).
(19 sts)
Continue to cable cast on from
the last stitch of the ear flap.
Cast on (18 sts 37 sts)
Transfer the second ear flap
(purl side facing) onto the
circular needle. (53 sts)
Continue to cable cast on from
the last stitch of the ear flap.
Cast on (2 sts 55 sts)
K 4 rounds.

Yarn B: K 1 round.
Yarn A: K 1 round.

Work from the snowflake chart, below, repeating the motif 5 times around for 9 rounds.

Snowflake Chart

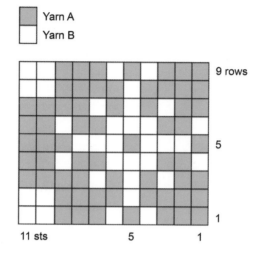

Yarn A: K 1 round.
Yarn B: K 1 round.
Yarn A: K 12 rounds.

Shape crown

1st round: (K9, K2tog) 5 times   (50 sts)
2nd round: (K8, K2tog) 5 times   (45 sts)
3rd round: (K7, K2tog) 5 times   (40 sts)
4th round: (K6, K2tog) 5 times   (35 sts)
5th round: (K5, K2tog) 5 times   (30 sts)
6th round: (K4, K2tog) 5 times   (25 sts)
7th round: (K3, K2tog) 5 times   (20 sts)
8th round: (K2, K2tog) 5 times   (15 sts)
9th round: (K1, K2tog) 5 times   (10 sts)
10th round: (K2tog) 5 times   (5 sts)
Break yarn and thread through remaining stitches.

To finish

Weave in all ends. Using yarn A make 2 chin ties as follows:

Cut 6 lengths of yarn of 60cm long. Holding the lengths together, find the centre point and use the crochet hook to pull a few centimetres of the centre point through the bottom of the ear flap to create a loop.

Draw ends through the loop and tighten to secure.

Divide the resulting 12 strands into three sections of 4 strands each and plait to about 16cm long.

Take the remaining length and wrap it in around your index finger and back through the loop created to make a knot to secure the plait.

Trim the tassel so that all the ends are the same length (the whole tie should be approx. 21cm long).

Repeat for the second earflap.

Bow Headband

MATERIALS

Grannies, Inc. Ever So Soft DK
Yarn (100% merino wool)
Colourway 1 (opposite)
• A: 1 x 50g hank Corn
• B: 1 x 50g hank Oyster
Colourway 2 (page 129)
• A: 1 x 50g hank Aubergine
1 pair of UK size 11 (3mm) needles
1 set of UK size 10.5 (3.5mm)
double-pointed needles

1 x 5cm wide elastic hairband
headband

TENSION

23 sts and 36 rows to 10cm
measured over st st using UK size
11 (3mm) needles.

MEASUREMENTS

One size fits all.

Pattern

To make the bow
Yarn A: Using 3mm needles, cast on 45 sts.
Row 1: K.
Row 2: P.
(Rows 1 and 2 make up st st).

Continue in st st until the work measures 14cm from cast-on edge, then cast off.

Fold the work over lengthwise with right sides outwards and, using mattress stitch, seam the joining side edges. Then seam the cast-on and off edges and press using a cool iron over a damp cloth to create a double-thick rectangle of approximately 8 x 14cm.

To make the centre of the bow
[Colourway 1: *Yarn B;* Colourway 2: *Yarn A*]

Using 3mm needles, cast on 6 stitches.

Continue in st st until the work measures 7cm from the cast-on edge and cast off.

To make the headband...
[Colourway 1: *Yarn B;* Colourway 2: *Yarn A*]

Using 3.5mm double-pointed needles, make a 5-stitch i-cord (see page 107 for instructions) approximately 50cm long when stretched and cast off. Fold one end of the i-cord back on itself around the elastic hairband and join using back stitch. Repeat at the other end of the cord to incorporate the hairband at either end to allow the headband to fit comfortably around the head without slipping off.

Repeat the instructions to make a second cord and attach it to the same hairband to make a 2-cord headband.

To finish

Gather the bow rectangle in the centre and wrap around a length of yarn 3 or 4 times, securing with a treble knot at the back of the bow and leaving two long tails for use in positioning the bow later on. Holding both cords against the back of the bow, wrap the bow centrepiece around the cords and bow where it is gathered in the middle. Seam the cast-on and off edges of the bow centrepiece.

Use the tails from the bow gathering to secure the bow to the cord slightly to one side of the centre so that the bow will sit to the side when worn. Weave in all ends neatly and block (see page 87).

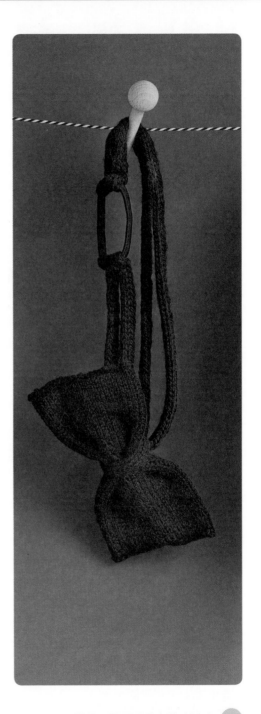

Berry Beret

MATERIALS
Grannies, Inc. Ever So Soft DK
Yarn (100% merino wool)
• 1 x 50g hank Crimson
1 pair of UK size 8 (4mm) needles

TENSION
22 sts and 28 rows to 10cm
measured over st st using UK
size 8 (4mm) needles.

MEASUREMENTS
One size fits all.

Pattern

Cast on 106 sts.
Row 1: K2 (P2, K2) to end.
Row 2: P2 (K2, P2) to end.
(Rows 1 and 2 make up 2 x 2 rib.)
Work 6 more rows in 2 x 2 rib.
Inc row: *inc in next st, K3, rep from * to last 2 sts, K1.   (133 sts)
P 1 row.
Row 1: (RS): *K1, K2tog, yf, K1, yf, K2tog tbl, rep from * to last st, K1.
Row 2 and every following alt row: P.
Row 3: K2tog, *yf, K3, yf, (sl 1) twice, K1, p2sso, rep from * to last 5 sts,
    yf, K3, yf, K2tog tbl.
Row 5: *K1, yf, K2tog tbl, K1, K2tog, yf, rep from * to last st, K1.

Row 7: K2, *yf, (sl 1) twice, K1, p2sso, yf, K3, rep from * to last 5 sts, yf, (sl 1) twice, K1, p2sso, yf, K2.

Row 8: P.

These 8 rows form the pattern. Continue as set until the work measures 20cm from cast-on edge.

Shape crown

Row 1: K2tog, *K3, sl 1, K2tog, psso, rep from * to last 5 sts, K3, K2tog. (89 sts)

Rows 2, 3 and 4: Work 3 rows st st.

Row 5: K1, *sl 1, K2tog, psso, K1, rep from * to end. (45 sts)

Rows 6, 7 and 8: Work 3 rows st st.

Row 9: (K2, K2tog) to last st, K1.   (34 sts)

Rows 10, 11 and 12: Work 3 rows st st.

Row 13: (K1, K2tog) to last st, K1.   (23 sts)

Row 14: P.

Row 15: (K2tog) to last st, K1.   (12 sts)

Row 16: (P2tog) to end.   (6 sts)

Break yarn, thread through the remaining stitches and fasten off.

To finish

Weave in all ends and block (see page 87).

Super Snood

MATERIALS

Grannies, Inc. Ever So Warm
Chunky Yarn (100% merino wool)
- A: 5 x 50g hanks Spearmint
- B: 1 x 50g hank Lightning
1 pair of UK size 000 (10mm)
circular needles, any length greater
than 80cm

TENSION

7 sts and 11 rows to 10cm
measured over brioche st using
UK size 000 (10mm) needles.

MEASUREMENTS

Approx. 18 x 115cm.

Pattern

Use circular needles to knit flat (the length is needed to hold the desired number of stitches not for circular knitting).

Yarn A: Cast on 150 sts.
Row 1: K2, *yo, sl1, K1, rep from * to last 2 sts, K2.
Row 2: P2, *yo, sl1, K2tog, rep from * to last 2 sts, P2. (Note that when you K2tog you will be knitting the sl1 together with the yo of the previous row.)
(Row 2 makes up brioche st.)
Continue in brioche st for another 9 rows.
Yarn B: Continue in brioche st for another 2 rows.
Yarn A: Continue in brioche st for another 4 rows.
Last row: P2, *P1, K2tog, rep from * to last 2 sts, P2.

Cast off as loosely as you can, knitwise for the first and last 2 sts and in 1x1 rib pattern on the sts between.

To finish

Weave in all ends neatly but do not block. Fold piece in half so that the 2 side seams meet and join using mattress stitch.

Two-Gauge Garter Scarf

MATERIALS

Grannies, Inc. Ever So Soft DK
Yarn (100% merino wool)
- A: 2 x 50g hanks Oyster
- B: 2 x 50g hanks Mink
1 pair of UK size 0 (8mm) needles
1 pair of 15mm needles

TENSION

11 sts and 15 rows to 10cm
measured over 2-gauge garter
pattern using 8mm and 15mm
needles and 2 strands of yarn.

MEASUREMENTS

Approx. 16 x 200cm.

Pattern

Use 1 strand of yarn A and 1 strand of yarn B together throughout.
Using 8mm needles, cast on 18 sts.
*Row 1: K 1 row.
Row 2: K 1 row.
Row 3: K 1 row.

Change to 15mm needles.
Row 4: K 1 row.
Change back to 8mm needles.
Repeat the four rows from * until work measures 200cm from cast-on
edge and cast off.

To finish

Add tassels as follows:
Make 36 tassels (18 for each end) as follows and space them 1 stitch apart along each end of the scarf.

Cut 2 lengths of yarn (1 mink, 1 oyster) each 28cm long, align and fold in half, making a loop. Pull the loop through the scarf edge between the cast-on/off stitches and the first row from front to back (a crochet hook can help with this). Slip the tassel ends through the loop at the back and pull tightly to create a neat knot at the scarf's edge.

Weave in all ends neatly and block (see page 87).

Diamond Scarf

MATERIALS

Grannies, Inc. Ever So Warm
Chunky Yarn (100% merino wool)
• 4 x 50g hanks Turquoise
1 pair of UK size 0 (8mm) needles

TENSION

12 sts and 18 rows to 10cm
measured over st st using UK
size 0 (8mm) needles.

MEASUREMENTS

Approx. 20 x 160cm.

Pattern

Cast on 26 sts.

K 2 rows.

Row 1: K1, *K2, K2tog, yon, K3, rep from * to end of row, K1.

Row 2: K1, *P1, P3tog, tbl, yon, P1, yon, P2tog, P1, rep from * to end of row, K1.

Row 3: *K2 tog, yon, K3, yon, sl 1, K1, psso, rep from * to end of row, K1.

Row 4: K1, P to last st, K1.

Row 5: K1, *yon, sl 1, K1, psso, K5, rep from * to last st, k1.

Row 6: K1,*yon, P2tog, P2, P2tog tbl, yon, P1, rep from * to last st, k1.

Row 7: K1, *K2, yon, sl 1, K1, psso, K2tog, yon, K1, rep from * to last st, K1.

Row 8: K1, P to last st, K1.

These 8 rows form the pattern. Continue as set until the work measures 160cm from cast-on edge.

Cast off.

To finish

Weave in all ends neatly and block (see page 87).

Cosy Collar

MATERIALS

Grannies, Inc. Ever So Soft DK
Yarn (100% merino wool)
• A: 1 x 50g hank Aubergine
1 pair of UK size 2 (7mm) circular
needles, 40cm length
1 pair of UK size 0 (8mm) circular
needles, 40cm length

TENSION

12 sts and 18 rows to 4in (10cm)
measured over st st using UK size
0 (8mm) needles.

MEASUREMENTS

Approx. 20cm wide x 44cm long.

Pattern

Using 7mm circular needles cast on 51 sts.
1st round: *K1, P2, rep from * to end.
(Row 1 makes up 1x2 rib.)
Continue in 1x2 rib until work measures 4cm from cast-on edge.

Change to 8mm circular needles.
Next round: K
Next round: P
(Last 2 rounds make up st st.)
Continue in st st until work measures 38cm from cast-on edge.
Continue in 1x2 rib until work measures 42cm from cast-on edge.
Cast off very loosely.

To finish

Weave in all ends neatly and block.

Lacy Cape

MATERIALS

Grannies, Inc. Ever So Soft DK
Yarn (100% merino wool)
• 3 x 50g hanks Mink
1 pair of UK size 8 (4mm) needles
1 button

TENSION

22 sts and 28 rows to 10cm
measured over st st using UK
size 8 (4mm) needles.

MEASUREMENTS

Approx. 25 x 90cm.

Pattern

Cast on 185 sts.

K 2 rows.

Row 1: (K2), K1, *yon, K2tbl, place st on left-hand needle, pass next st
over it and replace on right-hand needle, yon, K5, rep from * to last 4
sts, yon, K2 tbl and pass st over as before, yon, K1, (K2).

Continue to follow pattern, keeping K2 at beg and end of each row for garter st border.

Row 2 and foll alternate rows: P.

Row 3: As row 1.

Row 5: K1, *K3, yon, sl 1, K1, psso, K1, K2tog, yon, rep from * to last 4 sts, K4.

Row 7: K1, *yon, K2tbl and pass st over as before, yon, K1, rep from * to last 4 sts, yon, K2tbl and pass st over as before, yon, K1.

Repeat these 8 rows until the work measures approx. 24cm from cast-on edge, ending with a full repeat.

K 2 rows.

Cast off.

To finish

Weave in all ends neatly and block (see page 87). Sew the button at the top corner.

Utility Wrist Warmers

MATERIALS

Grannies, Inc. Ever So Soft DK
Yarn (100% merino wool)
• 1 x 50g hank Corn
1 pair of UK size 8 (4mm) needles
6 buttons

TENSION

18 sts and 29 rows to 10cm
measured over st st using UK
size 8 (4mm) needles.

MEASUREMENTS

Approx. 6.5 x 32cm.

Pattern

Cast on 45 sts.
Row 1: *K1, P1, rep from * to last st, K1.
Row 2: *P1, K1, rep from * to last st, P1.
(Row 1 and 2 make up 1x1 rib)
Continue in 1x1 rib until the work measures 40cm from cast-on edge
and cast off.

Repeat instructions for the second wrist warmer.

To finish

Weave in all ends neatly. Fold the piece in half lengthwise and seam using mattress stitch for 5cm from the bottom edge. Leave a 4cm

thumbhole and continue to seam to the top edge.

Fold the arm opening edge back by approximately 8cm and sew on
3 buttons in a row on the opposite side to the thumb opening.

Repeat finishing instructions for the second wrist warmer.

Fingerless Gloves

MATERIALS
Grannies, Inc. Ever So Soft DK
Yarn (100% merino wool)
• 1 x 50g hank Oyster
1 pair of UK size 8 (4mm) needles
1 m ribbon

TENSION
23 sts and 32 rows to 10cm
measured over st st using UK
size 8 (4mm) needles.

MEASUREMENTS
Approx. 18cm long.

Pattern

Instructions for lace panel

Row 1: (RS): K.

Row 2 and every following alternate row: P.

Row 3: K.

Row 5: K4, K2tog, YF, K1, YF, sl 1, K1, psso, K4.

Row 7: K3, K2tog, YF, K3, YF, sl 1, K1, psso, K3.

Row 9: K2 (K2tog, YF) twice, K1, (YF, sl 1, K1, psso) twice, K2.

Row 11: K1 (K2tog, Yf) twice, K3, (YF, sl 1, K1, psso) twice, K1.

Row 13: (K2tog, YF) 3 times, K1, (YF, sl 1, K1, psso) 3 times.

Row 14: P.

Right-hand glove

*Cast on 43 sts.

Work 5 rows garter st.

Starting with a K row, work 6 rows st st.

Eyelet row: K3, (K2tog, YF, K3) to end.

Starting with a P row, work 5 rows st st. *

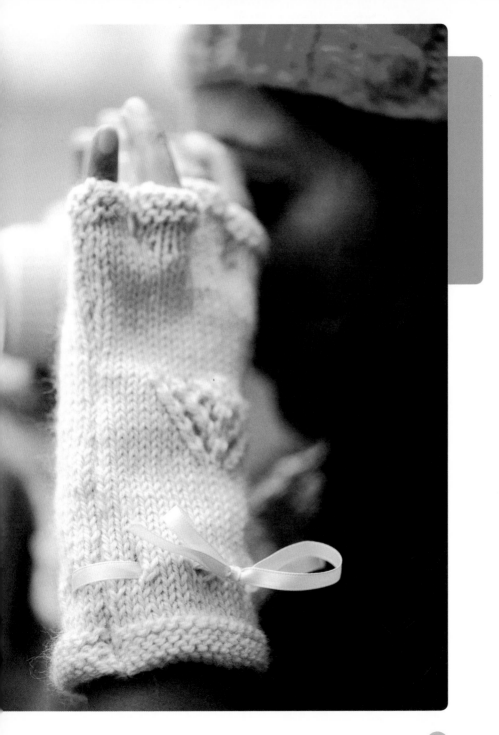

Shape thumb gusset

Row 1: K23, M1, K1, M1, K19. (45 sts)

Row 2 and every following alt row: P.

Row 3: K.

Row 5: K23, M1, K3, M1, K19. (47 sts)

Row 9: K5, work row 5 of 13 st lace panel, K5, M1, K5, M1, K19. (49 sts)

Row 11: K5, work row 7 of lace panel, K to end.

Row 13: K5, work row 9 of lace panel, K5, M1, K7, M1, K19. (51 sts)

Row 15: K5, work row 11 of lace panel, K to end.

Row 17: K5, work row 13 of lace panel, K5, M1, K9, M1, K19. (53 sts)

Row 19: K to end.

Row 21: K23, M1, K11, M1, K19. (55 sts)

Row 22: P.

Divide for thumb

K36, turn, cast on 1 st, P14.

Starting with a K row, work 3 rows st st.

Work 3 rows garter st.

Cast off.

Join thumb seam

With RS facing, pick up and K 1 st from base of thumb, K to end. (43 sts)

**P 1 row, work 8 rows st st.

1st finger

K28, turn, cast on 1 st, P13, turn, cast on 1 st.

Work 3 rows st st on these 14 sts.

With WS facing, work 3 rows garter st.

Cast off.

Join seam.

2nd finger

With RS facing, join yarn and pick up and K 2 sts from base of 1st finger, K5, turn, cast on 1 st, P13, turn, cast on 1 st. (14 sts)

Work 5 rows st st.

With WS facing, work 3 rows garter st.

Cast off.

Join seam.

3rd finger

With RS facing, join yarn and pick up and K 2 sts from base of 2nd finger, K5, turn, cast on 1 st, P13, turn, cast on 1 st, complete as for 1st finger.

4th finger

With RS facing, join yarn and pick up and K 1 st at base of 3rd finger, K to end.

P 1 row. (12 sts)

Complete 12 as for 1st finger.

Join side seam. **

Left-hand glove

Work as for right-hand glove from * to *.

Shape thumb gusset

Row 1: K19, M1, K1, M1, K23. (45 sts)

Row 2 and every following alt row: P.

Row 3: K.

Row 5: K19, M1, K3, M1, K23. (47 sts)

Row 7: K.

Row 9: K19, M1, K5, M1, K5, work row 5 of lace panel, K5. (49 sts)

Row 11: K31, work row 7 of lace panel, K5.

Row 13: K19, M1, K7, M1, K5, work pattern row 9 of lace panel, K5. (51 sts)

Row 15: K33, work row 11 of lace panel, K5.

Row 17: K19, M1, K9, M1, K5, work row 13 of lace panel, K5 (53 st)
Row 19: K to end.
Row 21: K19, M1, K19, M1, K23. (55 sts)
Row 22: P.

Divide for thumb
K32, turn, cast on 1 st, P14.
Starting with a K row, work 3 rows st st.
Work 3 rows garter st.
Cast off.

Join thumb seam
With RS facing, join yarn and pick up and K 1 st from base of thumb,
K to end. 43 sts.
Complete as for right-hand glove from ** to **.

To finish

Weave in all ends neatly and block (see page 87). Thread half the length
of the ribbon around the eyelets of the right-hand glove and tie in a
bow and trim as required. Repeat for left-hand glove.

Mittens

MATERIALS

Grannies, Inc. Ever So Warm
Chunky Yarn (100% merino
wool)
• A: 3 x 50g hank Olive
1 pair of UK size 1 (7.5mm)
needles
1 pair of UK size 00 (9mm)
needles

TENSION

12 sts and 16 rows to 10cm
measured over st st using UK
size 00 (9mm) needles.

MEASUREMENTS

One size fits all.

Pattern

Using 7.5mm needles, cast on 26 sts.
Row 1: *K2, P2, rep from * to last 2 sts, K2.
Row 2: *P2, K2, rep from * to last 2 sts, K2.
Repeat these 2 rows 4 times more, then row 1 once more.
Next row: K1 (inc in next 2 sts, P2) 6 times, K1. (38 sts)

Change to 9mm needles and work pattern:
Row 1: K.
Row 2 and every second row: K1, P to last st, K1.
Row 3: K1, *K2, C4B, rep from * to last st, K1.
Row 5: K.

Row 7: K1, *C4F, K2, rep from *to last st, K1.
Row 8: K1, P to last st, K1.
These 8 rows set the pattern. Keeping continuity work as follows...

Shape thumb gusset
Row 9: K1, patt 14 sts, M1, K8, M1, patt 14 sts. (40 sts)
Rows 10 and 12: K1, P to last st, K1.
Row 11: K1, patt 14 sts, K10, patt 14 sts, K 1.
Row 13: K1, patt 14 sts, M1, K10, patt 14 sts, K1. (42 sts)
Row 14: As row 2.
Row 15: Divide for thumb as follows: K1, (C4F, K2) x 2, K14, turn, P12.
Work 6 rows st st on these 12 sts.
Next row: K2tog to end. Break off yarn and thread through these 6 sts.
Pull up tightly and join row ends to base of thumb.
With RS facing, join yarn and pick up 2 sts from base of thumb and
pattern across 14 sts as follows. (K2, C4F) x 2, K3. 32 sts.
Row 16: As row 2.
Rows 17–28: Work rows 1–8 once more then rows 1–4 once more.
Row 29: K1, sl 1, K1, psso, K11, K2tog, sl 1, K1, Psso, K11, K2tog, K1.
   (28 sts)

Shape top
Row 30: As row 2.
Row 31: K1, sl1, K1, psso, K1, C4F, K4, K2tog, sl1, K1, psso, C4f, K5,
K2tog, K1. (24sts)
Row 32: K1, P2tog, P7, P2tog tbl, P2tog, P7, P2tog tbl, K1. (20 sts)
Cast off.
Repeat instructions for the second mitten.

To finish

Weave in all ends neatly and block (see page 87). Horizontally seam the
top of each mitten and side seams using mattress stitch.

Dancing Legwarmers

MATERIALS

Grannies, Inc. Ever So Warm
Chunky Yarn (100% merino wool)
• 4 x 50g hanks Hot Pink
1 pair of UK size 0 (8mm) needles

TENSION

12 sts and 18 rows to 10cm
measured over st st using UK
size 0 (8mm) needles.

MEASUREMENTS

Approx. 40cm long x 34cm
circumference.

Pattern

Cast on 37 sts.
Row 1: *K2, P2, rep from * to last st, K1.
Row 2: *P1, *K2, P2, rep from * to end.
(Rows 1 and 2 make up 2x2 rib.)
Work in 2x2 rib for another 2 rows.

Row 1 (RS): *K1, K2tog, yf, K1, yf, K2tog tbl, rep from * to last st, K1.
2nd and every alternate row: P.
Row 3: K2tog, *yf, K3, yf, [sl 1] twice, K1, p2sso, rep from * to last 5 sts,
    yf, K3, yf, K2tog tbl.
Row 5: *K1, yf, K2tog tbl, K1, K2tog, yf, rep from * to last st, K1.
Row 7: K2, *yf, [sl 1] twice, K1, p2sso, yf, K3, rep from * to last 5 sts, yf,
    [sl 1] twice, K1, p2sso, yf, K2.
Row 8: P.
Repeat these 8 rows as set until the work measures approx 37.5cm long,
ending with a full repeat.

Work 4 rows 2x2 rib.
Cast off.

Repeat instructions for the second legwarmer.

To finish

Weave in all ends neatly and block. Fold the piece in half lengthwise
and seam sides using mattress stitch.

Repeat finishing instructions for the second legwarmer.

Slouch Socks

MATERIALS
Grannies, Inc. Ever So Soft DK
Yarn (100% merino wool)
• 3 x 50g hanks Mediterranean
1 pair of UK size 8 (4mm) needles
1.5m ribbon

TENSION
23 sts and 32 rows to 10cm
measured over st st using UK
size 8 (4mm) needles.

MEASUREMENTS
One size fits all.

Pattern

Instructions for lace panel

Row 1: (RS): K2, K2tog, YF, K2tog but do not slip from needle, K the 1st
of these 2 sts again, then slip both sts from the needle together, YF, sl
1, K1, psso, K2.

Row 2: P.

Row 3: K1, K2tog, YF, K4, YF, sl 1, K1, psso, K1.

Row 4: P.

Row 5: K2tog, YF, K1, K2tog (YF)twice, sl 1, K1, psso, Yf, sl 1, K1, psso.

Row 6: P4, K1 into 1st YF, P1 into 2nd YF, P4.

Row 7: K2, Yf, sl 1, K1, psso, K2, K2tog, YF, K2.

Row 8: P.

Row 9: K3, Yf, sl 1 , K1, psso, K2tog, Yf, K3.

Row 10: P.

Repeat these 10 rows.

For the socks

Cast on 70 sts.

Row 1: K 2, *P2, K2, rep from * to end.

Row 2: P2, *K2, P2, rep from * to end.

Rep these 2 rows 3 times more.

Eyelet row: K2, K2tog, *YF, K5, K2tog, rep from * to last 3 sts, YF, K3.

Row 1: K28, P2, work row 1 of lace panel, P2, K28.

Row 2: P28, K2, work row 2 of lace panel, K2, P28.

These 2 rows set the pattern. Continue to follow the instructions for the panel until 5 complete repeats have been worked.

Shape lower leg

Row 1: K5, skpo, K21, P2, patt 10, P2, K21, K2tog, K5. 68 sts.

Row 2: P27, K2, patt 10, K2, P27.

Row 3: K5, skpo, K20, P2, patt 10, P2, K20, K2tog, K5. 66 sts.

Row 4: P26, K2, patt 10, K2, P26.

Work 2 more dec rows as set, finishing with RS facing. 62 sts.

Continue to work straight until 8 complete lace panel patterns have been worked in total, keeping continuity of pattern.

Shape lower foot

Row 1: K11, skpo, K11, P2, patt 10, P2, K11, K2tog, K11. 60 sts.

Rows 2–4: Work 3 rows straight, keeping continuity of pattern.

Row 5: K11, skpo, K10, P2, patt 10, P2, K10, K2tog, K11. 58 sts.

Rows 6–8: As rows 2–4.

Row 9: K11, skpo, K9, P2, patt 10, P2, K9, K2tog, K11. 56 sts.

Rows 10–12: As rows 2–4.

Row 13: K11, skpo, K8, P2, patt 10, P2, K8, K2tog, K11. 54 sts.

Row 14: As row 2.

Starting with row 5, work a further 16 pattern rows (11 complete patterns in total).

Work 2 rib rows (as rows 1 and 2 on ribbing at beg of pattern).

Shape toe

Row 1: Rib 12, skpo, K2tog, rib 22,
   skpo, K2tog, rib 12.
Row 2: Rib 12, P2, rib 22, P2, rib 12.
Row 3: Rib 11, skpo, K2tog, rib 20,
   skpo, K2tog, rib 11.
Row 4: Rib 11, P2, rib 20, P2, rib 11.

Continue to dec 4 sts in this
manner, keeping continuity of rib,
until 6 dec rows have been worked
and you have 30 sts remaining,
finishing with a WS row. Cast off.

Repeat instructions for the second
sock.

To finish

Weave in all ends neatly and block
(see page 87). Join back seam using
mattress st, then sew across toe with
foot and leg seam at centre.

Thread half the length of the ribbon around the eyelets of the first
sock and tie in a bow and trim as
required.

Repeat finishing instructions for the
second sock.

Wellie Socks

MATERIALS

Grannies, Inc. Ever So Warm
Chunky Yarn (100% merino wool)
• 7 x 50g hanks Chartreuse
1 pair of UK size 1 (7.5mm) needles
1 pair of UK size 0 (8mm) needles
1 pair of UK size 00 (9mm) needles
1 cable needle
1 spare needle or stitch holder

TENSION

12 sts and 16 rows to 10cm
measured over st st using UK size 00
(9mm) needles.

MEASUREMENTS

One size fits all (foot section can be
longer or shorter by increasing or
decreasing rows respectively).

Pattern

Sock tops

Using 9mm needles, cast on 10 sts.

K 1 row.

(RS) inc row: K1, P2, inc knitwise into next 4 sts, P2, K1. (14 sts)

Next row: K3, P8, K3.

Row 1: K1, P2, K8, P2, K1.

Row 2 and every following alt row: K3, P8, K3.

Rows 3 and 4: as rows 1 and 2.

Row 5: K1, P2, C8B, P2, K1.

Rows 7–10: Rep rows 1 and 2 twice.

Rep these 10 rows 4 times more.

Dec row: K1, P2. (K2tog) x 4, P2, K1. 10 sts.

K 1 row.

Cast off.

Main socks

With RS of sock top facing, pick up and K 47 sts evenly, along row ends using 9mm needles. Turn.

Row 1: (RS facing): K1, *K3, P3, rep from * to last 4 sts, K4.

Row 2: K1, *P3, K3, rep from * to last 4 sts, P3, K1.

Rep these 2 rows until the work measures 15cm from pick up row.

Change to 8mm needles and work a further 10cm rib.

** Change to 7.5mm needles and work a further 10cm rib** .

Divide for heel

Break off yarn and slip 1st 12 sts onto 7.5mm RH needle, slip next 23 sts onto st holder. Place remaining 12 sts onto spare needle. Turn. With WS facing, rejoin yarn to edges of 1st 12 sts, P2tog, P10, turn spare needle round, P10, P2tog. 22 sts.

Work as follows:

Row 1: K1, *sl 1, K1, rep from * to last st, K1.

Row 2: P.

Rep these last 2 rows 5 times more, placing a coloured marker at the centre of the last row. Turn heel as follows:

Row 1: K12, sl 1, K1, psso, K1.

Row 2: P4, P2tog, P1, turn.

Row 3: K5, sl 1, K1, psso, K1, turn.

Row 4: P6, P2tog, P1, turn.

Continuing in this manner, dec until 14 sts remain.

Next row: K11, sl 1, K1, psso, turn, P11, P2 tog, turn. 12 sts.

Break off yarn.

Lower foot

With RS facing, rejoin yarn to instep. Pick up and K 8 sts evenly along row ends, K across 12 sts of heel. 28 sts.

Row 1: P.

Row 2: K1, sl 1, K1, psso, K to last 3 sts, K2tog, K1.

Rep these 2 rows 4 times more, then row 1 once more. 18 sts.

Cont in st st until lower foot measures 18cm from the coloured marker, at the start of the heel turning. (The length of foot can be adjusted here, allow 3cm for toe shaping.)

Shape lower toe
Row 1: K1, sl1, K1, psso, K to last 3 sts, K2tog, K1. 16 sts.
Row 2: P1, P2tog, P to last 3 sts, P2tog tbl, P1. 14 sts.
Rep last 2 rows once more, then row 1 once more. 8 sts.
P 1 row, leave sts on holder.

Upper foot
Rejoin yarn to 23 sts on holder, placing a marker at centre of 1st row, proceed as follows:
Next row: K2tog, K2, (P3, K3) to last 7 sts, P3, K2, K2tog. 21 sts.
Row 1: (WS): *P3, K3, rep from * to last 3 sts, P3.
Row 2: *K3, P3. Rep from * to last 3 sts, K3.
Work 7cm in rib from marker as set, finishing with row 2.
Next row: P2tog, P1, (K3, P3) to last 6 sts, K3, P2tog, P1. 19 sts.
Starting with row 2, cont in rib as set for a further 9cm, finishing with a WS row and dec 1 st at centre of last row. 18 sts.

Shape upper toe
Work as for lower toe. Cast off as follows: place right sides of sock together. With WS facing, P tog 1 st from each needle and cast off each st as it is worked.

Repeat instructions for the second sock.

To finish

Weave in all ends neatly but do not block. Join leg and foot seam using mattress st, reversing seam for top of sock. Join the WS of the sock top piece to the main sock top using the vertical to horizontal seaming method described on page 96. Fold top over.

Repeat finishing instructions for the second sock.

Reusable Shopper

MATERIALS

Grannies, Inc. Ever So Soft DK
Yarn (100% merino wool)
• 2 x 50g hanks Mediterranean
4 size UK size 9 (3.75mm) double-
pointed needles (DPNS)
1 pair of UK size 9 (3.75mm)
circular needles, length 40cm
1 pair of UK size 7 (4.5mm)
circular needles, length 40cm
1 pair of UK size 4 (6mm)
circular needles, length 60cm

1 3.5mm crochet hook.
*(Note: if you don't have all these size
needles, use what you have, graduating
the size of the needles as you go along)*

TENSION

Not crucial to the sizing of the bag.

MEASUREMENTS

Dependent on tension and needles used but approx. 35cm wide x
55cm high.

Pattern

*NOTE: The bag can be made bigger by working more stitches onto the
base and by working more rounds in the net body of the bag and by
changing the needles sizes.*

Base

Using 3.5mm crochet hook, make a slip knot, place onto the crochet
hook, work a further 6 chain, 7 chain in total. Join first and last chain
with a slip stitch.

Crochet cast on

Insert one double-pointed needle into the remaining loop (the first
stitch of the round), then insert the needle through the first chain and
wrap the working yarn around it to pick up one stitch. (2 sts on first
DPN.) With 2nd DPN, pick up 3 sts in the same way, working around the

crochet chains. With the 3rd DPN, pick up 3 sts. 8 sts in total.

Place a marker onto the 3rd DPN, this will mark the end of the round.

Alternative cast on

Use 2 of the DPNs and cast on 8 sts normally, transfer 3 sts onto the first DPN, 3 sts onto the 2nd DPN and leave the last 2 sts onto the 3rd DPN, join. Place a marker at the end.

NOTE: Working on the 3 needles the sts won't be equal but the pattern will not be affected. Remember to pull the last st of each round a little tighter so as not to have a ladder effect.

With the 4 DPNs, work the following:

Foundation round: Knit.

Round 1: *YO, K1: rep from*. 16 sts.

Round 2 and every alt round: Knit.

Round 3: *YO, K3, YO, K1: rep from*. 24 sts.

Round 5: *YO, K5, YO, K1: rep from*. 32 sts.

Round 7: *YO, K7, YO, K1: rep from*. 40 sts.

Round 9: *YO, K9, YO, K1: rep from *. 48 sts.

Continue to increase 8 sts on every other round with 2 YOs in each corner as set by the first 9 rounds till 112 sts have been made, ending with a knit round.

Change to the 40cm circular needle size 3.75mm when the DPNs start to get a bit crowded with sts.

Net body

Keeping the marker at the end of each round, work the following:

Foundation round: Knit.

Round 1: Sl1, K2tog, psso, yf, k1, yf.

Round 2: Knit.

Round 3: Yf, k1, yf, sl 1, K2tog, psso.

Round 4: Knit.

These 4 rounds form the pattern.

Change to 40cm circular needle size 4.5mm, continue working the 4 round pattern, repeat till 12 more rounds have been worked.

Change to 60cm circular needle, size 6mm, continue in pattern working a further 32 rounds or till you have reached your desired length, ending with a Knit round.

Top ribbing

Knit 2 rounds, decreasing 4 sts evenly on the first round. 108 sts.

Next round: K3, P3: to end.

Repeat this round 5 times more.

Handle

Still with same circular needle, rib first 9 sts, place these onto a holder, cast off next 45 sts, rib next 8 sts (9 sts on RH needle), place these sts onto a holder. Cast off the remaining sts. You are now left with 1 st left on RH needle, transfer the first 9 sts left on holder onto LH needle of circular needle, cast off 1 more st, rib across the 8 remaining sts (9 sts are now on RH needle), turn.

With WS of bag facing, change to 2 of the DPNs used for the base. Now working back and forth.

Next row (WS): Cast on 5 sts beg of row, K5, rib to end.

Next row: Cast on 5 sts beg of row, P5, rib to end. 19 sts in total.

Next row (WS): K5, P3, K3, P3, K5.

Next row: P5, K3, P3, K3, P5.

Repeat these last 2 rows till handle measures 46cm or your desired length, ending with RS facing for next row.

Cast off 5 sts at beg of next 2 rows, rib to end.

Transfer the 9 sts left on holder onto 2nd DPN, hold both DPNs together, grafting the sts.

Fasten off.

To finish

Weave in all ends neatly but do not block. Fold handle flaps to the inner side of the handle and join edges using mattress st. Sew each inner ends of the handle to the top of the ribbing.

Argyll Bag

MATERIALS

Grannies, Inc. Ever So Warm
Chunky Yarn (100% merino
wool)
- A: 2 x 50g hanks Ash
- B: 1 x 50g hanks Fuchsia
- C: 1 x 50g hanks Chartreuse

1 pair of UK size 0 (8mm)
needles
1 pair of bamboo bag handles

TENSION

12 sts and 18 rows to 10cm
measured over st st using UK
size 0 (8mm) needles.

MEASUREMENTS

Approx. 25cm deep x 23cm
wide.

Pattern

Side (make 2)
Using yarn A and 8mm needles, cast on 30 sts.
Purl 1 row.
Work from chart row 1 until row 14 has been completed, repeat these
14 rows once more, then row 1 and 2 again. 31 rows. Knit 1 row in
yarn A only.

Rib top
With WS facing for next row, work the following:
Row 1: P2, K2: rep to last 2 sts, P2.
Row 2: K2, P2: rep to last 2 sts, K2.
Work 3 more rows in rib as set.
With RS facing, cast off 3 sts, rib next 3 sts so that you have 4 sts on
RH needle, cast off next 16 sts with 1 st remaining on RH needle, rib
next 3 sts, (4 sts on RH needle).

Argyll Chart

Yarn A
Yarn B
Yarn C

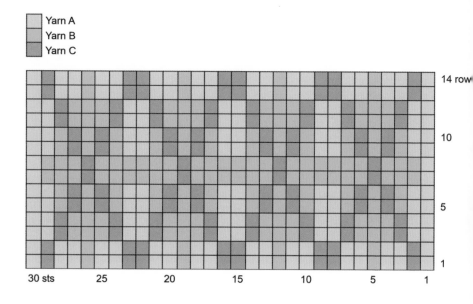

30 sts   25   20   15   10   5   1

14 row
10
5
1

Cast off remaining 3 sts. Fasten off.

With WS facing and working on the first block of 4 sts left on needle, work the following:

Row 1: K1, P2, K1.

Row 2: P1, K2, P1.

Repeat these 2 rows twice more.

Cast off in rib.

Rejoin yarn, repeat with the 2nd block of sts, cast off in rib.

To finish

Weave in all ends neatly and block. With the right sides of the bag facing outwards, sew the 3 sides using mattress stitch, taking the seam in by 1 st. Place handles folding the flaps of rib over each of the handle loops and sew in place to the inside of the bag.

Laptop Cozy

MATERIALS

Grannies, Inc. Ever So Warm
Chunky Yarn (100% merino wool)
- A: 3 x 50g hanks Ash
- B: 1 x 50g hank Hot Pink

1 pair of UK size 0 (8mm) needles
1 x 37cm long zip

TENSION

12 sts and 18 rows to 10cm
measured over st st using UK
size 0 (8mm) needles.

MEASUREMENTS

Approx. 27 x 37cm.

Pattern

NOTE: The laptop cover is worked using the Intarsia method using separate balls of yarn for each block of colour. Read chart from right to left on RS rows and from left to right on WS rows.

Front cover
Using yarn A and 8mm needles, cast on 46 sts.
Row 1: Knit.
Row 2: Purl.
Repeat last 2 rows twice more.
With RS facing for next row, place chart centrally as follows:
Row 1: K21 in yarn A, k4 in yarn B, k21 in yarn A.
Row 2: P20 in yarn A, p6 in yarn B, p20 in yarn A.
These 2 rows set the position of the chart only. Continue working in st st and following chart from row 3 until row 31 has been completed.
With WS facing for next row and working in yarn A only:
Row 1: Purl.
Row 2: Knit.

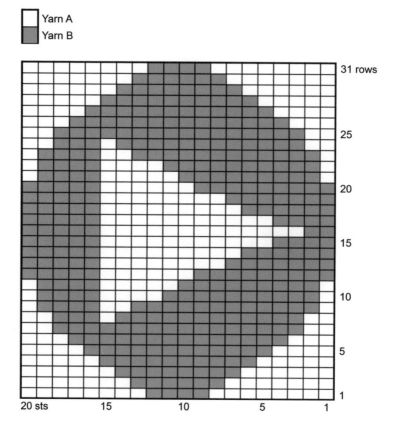

Yarn A
Yarn B

31 rows
25
20
15
10
5
1

20 sts 15 10 5 1

Repeat last 2 rows twice more ending with WS facing for next row.
Change to yarn B.
Purl 1 row.
Cast off purlwise.

Back cover
Using yarn A throughout and 8mm needles, cast on 46 sts.
Begin with a K row and work in st st for 43 rows.
With WS facing for next row, change to yarn B.
Purl 1 row.
Cast off purlwise.

To finish

Weave in all ends neatly and block (see page 87). Sew up the 3 sides of cover using mattress st leaving the top edge (yarn B edge) open. Place zip along this edge and sew in place.

iPod Cover

MATERIALS

Grannies, Inc. Ever So Soft DK
Yarn (100% merino wool)
• A: 1 x 50g hank Corn

Colour Option 1
• B: A scrap of Crimson
(approx. 2g)

Colour Option 2
• B: A scrap of Mediterranean
(approx. 2g)

1 pair of UK size 10 (3.25mm)
needles
1 pair of UK size 9 (3.75mm)
needles
1 button per cover

TENSION

24 sts x 30 rows over st st to 10cm
using 3.75mm needles.

MEASUREMENTS

Approx. 6cm wide x 11cm

Pattern

NOTE: iPod cover is knitted in st st with garter st edges. The front design is worked using the Intarsia method using separate lengths of yarn for each block of colour. Read chart from right to left on RS rows and from left to right on WS rows.

The cover is worked as one piece starting at top front edge and ending at top back edge.

Using yarn B and 3.25mm needles, cast on 16 sts.
Knit 4 rows.

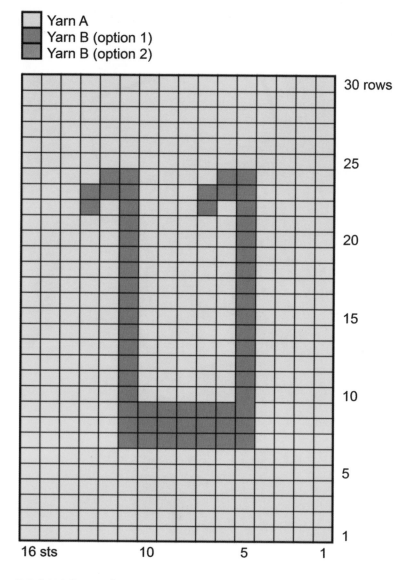

Yarn A
Yarn B (option 1)
Yarn B (option 2)

30 rows

25

20

15

10

5

1

16 sts   10   5   1

With RS facing for next row, change to 3.75mm needles and yarn A. Now follow the chart, changing the colours where indicated until row 30 has been worked. Place a marker at each end of last row.

Begin with a K row and yarn A, work in st st for a further 30 rows.

Edging and buttonhole flap

Using yarn B and 3.25mm needles:

Knit 5 rows.

Next row: Cast off 5 sts knitwise, K5 sts (6 sts on RH needle), leave these sts on a holder and cast off remaining sts, fasten off, turn.

With RS facing, rejoin yarn to remaining sts.

Knit 4 rows.

Next row: K2, cast off 2 sts, K1.

Next row: K2, cast on 2 sts, K2.

Knit a further 3 rows.

Cast off knitwise.

To finish

Weave in all ends neatly and block.

Fold cover in half at markers, sew up sides using mattress stitch. Sew on button to the front centre of garter st edging.

Needles Down, Feet Up

Stuff that wasn't Around in Our Day

YOUTUBE

Even the most talented of knitters can come across instructions in a pattern that they either haven't seen before or can't remember how to do. Along with comical clips of dogs on skateboards and choreographed wedding dances, YouTube is a fantastic free resource for knitters. You can search for pretty much any knitting term and you'll find loads of video tutorials on the subject. The tutorials will be of differing qualities, but generally the ones featured as 'top viewed' are the best.

RAVELRY

We at Grannies, Inc. love Ravelry.com, it is truly outstanding. It is an online community of knitters, crocheters, designers, spinners, weavers and dyers who chat to manage their craft and find inspiration. Log on and you'll find patterns, be able to create projects, keep notes, learn about different yarns and connect with other people in the craft community like never before. Membership is free, so we suggest you sign up and take a look around. You'll never look back.

YARN BOMBING

Although we would never encourage anyone to get involved in an illegal activity, we do think every knitter should be aware of a little art called 'yarn bombing' (AKA yarn storming). Though to have originated in Texas, USA, yarn bombing is a type of graffiti that is produced using yarn instead of spray paint and knitters instead of artists. Creative knitters are sneaking around the world covering, wrapping and dressing otherwise sterile public objects – such as phone boxes, trees and even the lions on London's Trafalgar Square – with knitted masterpieces whilst artistically using up all their yarn ends. So now that you know, try looking around you as you walk the streets and you might be lucky enough to spot some. Otherwise, a simple internet search will leave you marvelling at the astounding abilities of the most undercover of knitters.

KNITTING CIRCLES

Now we are not saying that knitting circles weren't around in our day, but boy have they changed! There are organised knitting circles going on in villages, towns and cities all over the world, so if you want to get social about your knitting, why not join your closest circle? Most circles will advertise themselves on the internet, but look out for posters in your local craft shop or ask around and you're sure to find something suitable. Usually held in cafés, pubs or public parks (if you're lucky enough with the weather), these circles are full of friendly folk who are ready and willing to teach the novice knitter or learn from the experienced. Failing that, they are just a great place to meet like-minded crafters and natter about whatever is bothering you that week.

If you want to get social with your knitting but can't find a local knitting circle, why not start one of your own? All you need to do is ask around for a suitable meeting place, decide on when and how often you will meet and advertise your circle any which way you can. Before you know it you'll be looking for a larger location or starting a second group to cater for the masses.

YARN FAIRS

There are lots of lovely yarn fairs held at different points during the year which are just a pleasure to visit as a knitter. We've put together a list of our favourites:

Name: Unravel
When: February
Where: Farnham, Surrey
Website: www.farnhammaltings.com

Name: Stitch and Craft Show
When: March
Where: Olympia, London
Website: www.stitchandcraft.co.uk

Name: Wonderwool Wales
When: April
Where: Builth Wells, Powys, Wales
Website: www.wonderwoolwales.co.uk

Name: Woolfest
Where: Cockermouth, Cumbria
When: June
Website: www.woolfest.co.uk

Name: Knit Nation
When: July
Where: South Kensington, London
Website: www.knitnation.co.uk

Name: I Knit London Weekender
When: September
Where: Waterloo, London
Website: www.iknit.org.uk

Name: The Knitting and Stitching Show
When: October and November
Where: London, Harrogate and Dublin
Website: www.twistedthread.com

Name: The Creative Crafts Shows
When: Various times throughout the year
Where: Various locations throughout the UK, check
the website for your nearest event
Website: www.sccshows.co.uk

Yarn details and substitutes

All of the patterns in this book are designed using one of Grannies, Inc.'s two merino wool yarns, one a DK weight and the other a chunky weight.

Name:	Ever So Soft DK		**Name:**	Ever So Warm Chunky
Brand:	Grannies, Inc.		**Brand:**	Grannies, Inc.
Weight:	DK		**Weight:**	Chunky
Meterage:	Approx. 125m		**Meterage:**	Approx. 50 m
Unit weight:	50 grams		**Unit weight:**	50 grams
Tension:	22 sts to 10cm		**Tension:**	11 sts to 10cm
Needle size:	4 mm (UK 8)		**Needle size:**	10 mm (UK 000)
Fibres:	100% Merino		**Fibres:**	100% Merino

We have taught you nothing if you think these two yarns are the only way to go! There is an amazing range of yarns out there that can be substituted into these patterns; the world is your oyster.

We've taken a look around and have suggested a few substitutes below however please don't let that stop you hunting around for your own (just be sure to read the section on 'Adapting Patterns to Different Yarns' on pages 28–9 before you do so).

SUBSTITUTES FOR GRANNIES, INC. EVER SO WARM CHUNKY YARN

Name:	DROPS Eskimo		**Name:**	Freedom 100% Wool
Brand:	Garnstudio		**Brand:**	Twilleys of Stamford
Weight :	Chunky		**Weight :**	Chunky
Meterage:	49 meters		**Meterage:**	49 meters
Unit weight:	50 grams		**Unit weight:**	50 grams
Tension:	10 sts to 10cm		**Tension:**	10 sts to 10cm
Needle size:	8-9mm (UK 0-00)		**Needle size:**	10 mm (UK 000)
Fibres:	100% Wool		**Fibres:**	100% Wool

Name: Freedom 100% Wool
Brand: Twilleys of Stamford
Weight : Chunky
Meterage: 49 meters
Unit weight: 50 grams
Tension: 10 sts to 10cm
Needle size: 10 mm (UK 000)
Fibres: 100% Wool

SUBSTITUTES FOR GRANNIES, INC. EVER SO SOFT DK YARN

Name: Pure Wool DK
Brand: Rowan
Weight : DK / 8 ply
Meterage: 124 meters
Unit weight: 50 grams
Tension: 22 sts to 10cm
Needle size: 3.75 - 4mm (UK 9-8)
Fibres: 100% Wool

Name: Merino Blend DK
Brand: King Cole
Weight : DK / 8 ply
Meterage: 112 meters
Unit weight: 50 grams
Tension: 22 sts to 10cm
Needle size: 4mm (UK 8)
Fibres: 100% Wool

Name: Rialto
Brand: Debbie Bliss
Weight : DK / 8 ply
Meterage: 105 meters
Unit weight: 50 grams
Tension: 22 sts to 10cm
Needle size: 3.75 - 4mm (UK 9-8)
Fibres: 100% Merino

Name: Cadenza
Brand: Colinette
Weight : DK / 8 ply
Meterage: 121 meters
Unit weight: 50 grams
Tension: 22 sts to 10cm
Needle size: 4mm (UK 8)
Fibres: 100% Merino

Acknowledgements

Although it may have felt sometimes that it was just little ol' me, locked in a small room, working away at this there are just so many people to thank for helping me put this book together. Firstly, thanks to Hannah Knowles at Ebury Press, who shared my vision for this book from the start and to the rest of the Ebury team for turning a load of words, illustrations and photos into the beautiful book it has become. Thanks to the wonderfully talented Sian Brown, for her help with the knitwear patterns and to Brent Darby for astounding me with his amazing photography of the samples by interpreting the tone of the book so perfectly.

A massive thank you to all the knitting grannies of Grannies, Inc for being such stars when it comes to turning people's designs into reality and for constantly surprising me with what they are capable of with a pair of needles and a ball of yarn!

A big hug goes to my mum for her constant support, to Ian for putting up with me, day in, day out and to the rest of my family and friends just for being who they are.

Lastly, thanks to my dad, who bought me the wool for my first knitting project. If only he'd have known where it would take me...

Index